WALKING THE WICKLOW WAY

A WEEK-LONG WALK FROM DUBLIN TO CLONEGAL

About the Author

Paddy Dillon is a prolific outdoor writer, with over 100 guidebooks to his name and contributions to 40 other titles. He has written for several outdoor magazines and other publications and has appeared on radio and television.

Paddy uses a tablet computer to write as he walks. His descriptions are therefore precise, having been written at the very point at which the reader uses them.

Paddy is an indefatigable long-distance walker who has walked all of Britain's National Trails and several European trails. He has also walked in Nepal, Tibet, Korea and the Rocky Mountains of Canada and the US. Paddy is a member of the Outdoor Writers and Photographers Guild and President of the Backpackers Club.

www.paddydillon.co.uk

Other Cicerone guides by the author

Glyndwr's Way
Mountain Walking in Mallorca
The Cleveland Way and the
 Yorkshire Wolds Way
The GR5 Trail
The GR20 Corsica
The Great Glen Way
The National Trails
The North York Moors
The Pennine Way
The Reivers Way
The South West Coast Path
The Teesdale Way (Martin Collins;
 updated by Paddy Dillon)
The Wales Coast Path
Trekking in Greenland – The Arctic
 Circle Trail
Trekking in Mallorca
Trekking in the Alps (contributing
 author)

Trekking in the Canary Islands
Walking and Trekking in Iceland
Walking in County Durham
Walking in Menorca
Walking in Sardinia
Walking in the Isles of Scilly
Walking in the North Pennines
Walking on Arran
Walking on Gran Canaria
Walking on Guernsey
Walking on Jersey
Walking on La Gomera and El
 Hierro
Walking on Lanzarote and
 Fuerteventura
Walking on La Palma
Walking on Madeira
Walking on Malta
Walking on Tenerife
Walking on the Azores

WALKING THE WICKLOW WAY

A WEEK-LONG WALK FROM DUBLIN TO CLONEGAL

by Paddy Dillon

JUNIPER HOUSE, MURLEY MOSS,
OXENHOLME ROAD, KENDAL, CUMBRIA LA9 7RL
www.cicerone.co.uk

© Paddy Dillon 2021
First edition 2021
ISBN: 978 1 78631 050 7

Printed in China on responsibly sourced paper on behalf of Latitude Press Ltd
A catalogue record for this book is available from the British Library.

Route mapping by Lovell Johns www.lovelljohns.com

Contains OpenStreetMap.org data © OpenStreetMap contributors, CC-BY-SA.
NASA relief data courtesy of ESRI
All photographs are by the author unless otherwise stated.

Updates to this guide

While every effort is made by our authors to ensure the accuracy of guide-books as they go to print, changes can occur during the lifetime of an edition. This guidebook was researched and written before the COVID-19 pandemic. While we are not aware of any significant changes to routes or facilities at the time of printing, it is likely that the current situation will give rise to more changes than would usually be expected. Any updates that we know of for this guide will be on the Cicerone website (www.cicerone.co.uk/1050/updates), so please check before planning your trip. We also advise that you check information about such things as transport, accommodation and shops locally. Even rights of way can be altered over time.

We are always grateful for information about any discrepancies between a guidebook and the facts on the ground, sent by email to updates@cicerone.co.uk or by post to Cicerone, Juniper House, Murley Moss, Oxenholme Road, Kendal, LA9 7RL.

Register your book: To sign up to receive free updates, special offers and GPX files where available, register your book at www.cicerone.co.uk.

Front cover: The prominent Great Sugar Loaf as seen from Knockree Youth Hostel

CONTENTS

ROUTE SUMMARY TABLE

Day	Stage	Distance	Ascent	Descent	Time
Day 1	Marlay Park to Knockree	20km (12½ miles)	650m (2130ft)	570m (1870ft)	6hr 30min
Day 2	Knockree to Oldbridge	21km (13 miles)	720m (2360ft)	650m (2130ft)	6hr 30min
Day 3	Oldbridge to Glendalough	9km (5½ miles)	300m (985ft)	400m (1310ft)	3hr
Day 4	Glendalough to Glenmalure	14km (8¾ miles)	460m (1510ft)	460m (1510ft)	4hr 30min
Day 5	Glenmalure to Moyne	23km (14¼ miles)	750m (2460ft)	720m (2360ft)	7hr 15min
Day 6	Moyne to Boley Bridge	23km (14¼ miles)	490m (1610ft)	540m (1770ft)	7hr 15min
Day 7	Boley Bridge to Clonegal	19.5km (12¼ miles)	400m (1310ft)	440m (1445ft)	6hr
Total distance	**Marlay Park to Clonegal**	**129.5km (80½ miles)**	**3770m (12,370ft)**	**3780m (12,400ft)**	**7 days**

Note that consistently choosing longer alternatives could add as much as 16km (10¼ miles) extra to the route, and detours off-route add even more.

Symbols used on route maps

~ route

-- alternative route

(S) start point

(F) finish point

(F) alternative finish point

> route direction

woodland

urban areas

railway

▲ peak

Λ campsite

■ building

church/monastery/cross

track

vehicle track

tarmac road

· other feature

Relief
in metres

800–1000

600–800

400–600

200–400

0–200

SCALE: 1:50,000

0 kilometres 0.5   1

0 miles   0.5

Contour lines are
drawn at 25m intervals
and highlighted at
100m intervals.

GPX files for all routes
can be downloaded free at
www.cicerone.co.uk/1050/GPX.

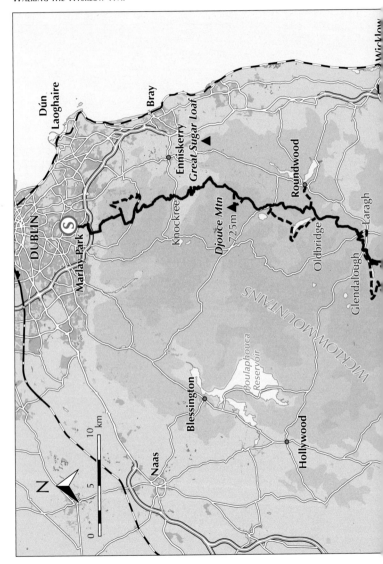

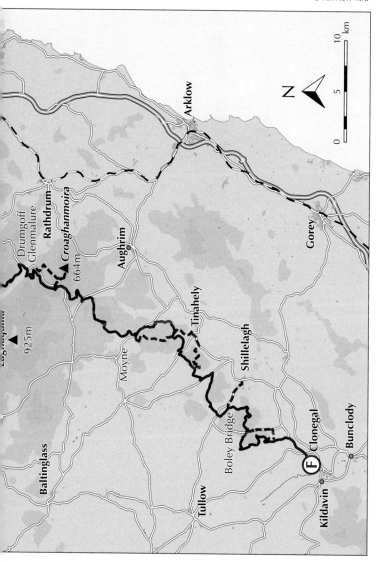

A prominent round tower stands in the 'Monastic City' at Glendalough (Day 3/Day 4)

INTRODUCTION

Walkers above the Dargle River, with Djouce Mountain beyond (Day 2)

The Wicklow Way is an ideal introduction to the network of trails in Ireland, being easy to reach, obvious to follow and full of interest. The Wicklow Way was the first waymarked long-distance walking trail to be established in Ireland, leaving Dublin and heading south through the Wicklow Mountains. The driving force behind the route was John James Bernard Malone, who was always referred to as JB Malone. He used to write for the *Evening Herald* and he later converted his newspaper articles into books about walking, with a particular emphasis on the history and heritage of the countryside. He first promoted the idea of a long walk through the Wicklow Mountains as early as 1966, although the route

wasn't officially opened until 1981, starting at Marlay Park on the southern outskirts of Dublin. It was a shorter route in those days, finishing at Moyne, but it was subsequently extended southwards to finish at Clonegal. My first encounter with the Wicklow Way was in 1982 and my correspondence with JB was brief, as he died in 1989. His memorial stone stands on the Wicklow Way above Luggala.

The route is mostly, but not entirely a 'Wicklow' way, because although the bulk of it is in Co Wicklow, it starts in Co Dublin and finishes in Co Carlow. After leaving Dublin city, the trail climbs quickly into the Dublin Mountains, and it soon becomes apparent that the route relies heavily on roads and forest tracks to cover most of its distance, although there are some fine paths across high heather moorlands. A succession of open hillsides and forested glens are crossed en route to Clonegal.

In recent years, several adjacent trails have been signposted and way-marked, and in some cases, these offer splendid alternatives to the main course of the Wicklow Way. Walkers can include nearby summits on clear days, enjoying extensive views that could well stretch to North Wales. The scenic Lough Dan can be explored, instead of following the Wicklow Way through a nearby forest. Villages with a range of facilities can be included for the sake of an hour's detour. The Miners' Way is a scenic and interesting alternative to a densely forested part of the Wicklow Way between Glendalough and Glenmalure. The entire course of the Wicklow Way is described from start to finish, but each day there are alternative routes that diverge from the main route and join again later, and these are included for their scenery, interest and variety.

Walkers can expect to spend about a week on the Wicklow Way, covering a minimum of 130km (80 miles). However, there are very few facilities actually on the route, so numerous detours off-route will ensure that anything up to 150 kilometres (93 miles) are more likely to be covered. While most people won't mind walking up to an hour off-route, anything longer seems excessive, so

some accommodation providers offer pick-up and drop-off services.

Since its inception, the bulk of walkers have followed the Wicklow Way from north to south, and all guidebooks have been written in that direction. There is no reason why the trail can't be followed from south to north, as the waymarking works just as well in reverse. However, care would be needed in order to re-interpret the route directions in reverse.

GEOLOGY

The geological history of the Wicklow Mountains begins 500 million years ago. There were no mountains. There was no Ireland. There was just the ancient Iapetus Ocean. Nearby land-masses were being eroded and volcanoes were erupting, so that the sea became filled with layer upon layer of sand, ash and mud, which hardened into sandstones and mudstones.

Around 420 million years ago, the European and North American continental plates collided, crushing and crumpling layers of rock upwards until they rose from the ocean as land. Deep within the rock, the heat and pressure were so intense that the rocks were transformed, with sandstones fusing into quartzite, while mudstones were converted into schist. Furthermore, the deeper part of the Earth's crust melted under the immense pressure, and a huge mass of molten rock formed a vast, deep-seated dome of magma, known as a batholith, that pushed the

Two Rock Mountain, or Fairy Castle, and its prominent cairn (Day 1, alternative route)

older rocks upwards under incredible pressure.

Where the molten magma found itself alongside the older rocks, molten materials and highly-pressured hot gases were forced into cracks, eventually solidifying into mineral veins, and the older rocks closest to the batholith were baked by the heat and transformed into what is known as a metamorphic aureole. The magma never broke the surface, but remained underground and cooled slowly into distinctive crystalline granite, formed of visible crystals of quartz, feldspar, mica and other minerals.

Over hundreds of millions of years, as Ireland itself finally took shape, with weathering and glaciation scouring away the landscape, the dome of ancient rocks was worn away, exposing the huge mass of granite beneath. Evidence of glaciation can be seen in the many steep-sided U-shaped glens, bowl-like corries, some containing little lakes, along with masses of ill-sorted rubble and boulder-strewn moraine.

The Wicklow granite is the largest mass of granite in both Ireland and Britain. Only tiny remnants of the original 'roof' of the dome that once covered the granite can be seen today, most notably as the schist cap on top of the highest mountain – Lugnaquilla. The main granite massif is surrounded by the older rocks, with Djouce Mountain being a notable peak of schist and the Great Sugar Loaf being a notable quartzite peak. The rich mineral veins were plundered to release their wealth between 1800 and 1963, yielding lead, zinc, copper, silver and even a little gold.

The waymarked Miners' Way visits several interesting mining sites and conveniently links with the course of the Wicklow Way.

SCENERY

Granite, schist and quartzite form rather poor soils, and as the Wicklow Mountains are consistently high, snagging the damp maritime airstream, the exposed and extensive uplands are notoriously bleak and boggy, spending a considerable amount of time covered by damp mist. While Co Wicklow is known as the 'Garden of Ireland', the main feature of the higher mountains is the brief summer flush of purple generated by blooming heather, otherwise visitors should look to the glens and lower hills for colour, including the bright yellow blaze of gorse bushes and rich green growth. The Wicklow Way only occasionally climbs high, and while it sometimes leads onto high and exposed slopes, it also spends a lot of time in the shelter of commercial forests, or follows roads and tracks through gentle pastoral country, dotted with farms, where rampant hedgerows are often filled with flowers. There are wooded areas, lakes and rivers, so overall the scenery is quite varied and enjoyable.

HISTORY

It is a futile exercise to try and condense the history of Ireland, often intensely and turbulently tied with the history of Britain, into a few short paragraphs, but it is worth making some basic points by concentrating mostly on Dublin and the Wicklow Mountains.

One thing worth bearing in mind is that, before the arrival of humans, Ireland was well-wooded and some remarkable beasts roamed through the countryside. The animal once referred to as the Irish Elk is now referred to as the Great Irish Deer (*Megaloceros giganteus*). It had immense antlers. Ireland's woodlands have been plundered by people for centuries, leaving Ireland one of the most sparsely-wooded countries in Europe. One of the last great woodlands is represented by a mere shadow of itself at Coolattin, near the village of Shillelagh in Co Wicklow. Hardly any self-generating ancient woodlands are left, and as coniferous tree species actually became extinct in Ireland, the extensive coniferous forests now blanketing parts of Co Wicklow are entirely recent and this is now the most forested part of Ireland.

In the distant past, Ireland was controlled by Celtic chieftains who generally accepted the authority of a High King. It was customary for chieftains to meet with the High King after travelling from various parts of Ireland to the Hill of Tara, well to the northwest of Dublin. (Bear in mind that Dublin city didn't exist at the time.) Those chieftains who passed through what ultimately became Co Wicklow followed a traditional route known as the *Slighe Cualann*, whose modern spelling is *Slí Cualann*. Remember this, as the Wicklow Way's Irish name is *Slí Cualann Nua*, meaning a 'new' version of the old Celtic route. This name is used on bilingual signposts along the length of the trail. The literal translation of 'Wicklow Way' into Irish would be *Slí Chill Mhantáin*, but this is not the accepted name, though for some peculiar reason it appears as such on Ordnance Survey maps. Perhaps someone at the Ordnance Survey wasn't paying attention!

Notable points in Irish history include the arrival of Christian missionaries from the 5th century, most notably the Romano-British St Patrick. Celtic Christianity favoured secluded rural retreats, such as the Monastic City at Glendalough. Christianity flourished in Ireland, at the same time as Christianity on the continent was suffering internal schisms and apparently endless strife with non-Christian cultures. The Vikings often targeted monasteries and churches, starting in the 8th century, and by the 9th century they dug in their heels and laid the foundations of the city of Dublin. The Vikings had very little influence or interest in the Wicklow Mountains.

Ireland's rural style of monasticism was eclipsed following the Anglo-Norman invasion of Ireland, from the 12th century. The Normans favoured large-scale monasteries and abbeys, and controlled land in a way that was foreign to the native Irish. Despite many Norman settlers

An arched window in the ruined Cathedral at Glendalough (Day 3/Day 4)

inter-marrying with the Irish and becoming 'more Irish than the Irish themselves', the way was already being paved for centuries of Anglo-Irish strife.

The phrase 'beyond the Pale' originated in Ireland and is particularly relevant in terms of Dublin and its relationship to the Wicklow Mountains. The 'Pale' was a rather fluid area of English control and influence that extended for some distance beyond Dublin. While the 'Pale' often extended beyond Drogheda and occasionally went as far north as Dundalk, it didn't extend too far across the plains into Co Kildare. The southern boundaries, however, finished abruptly far short of the

Wicklow is the most forested county in Ireland

Wicklow Mountains, where Irish chieftains remained resolute and the terrain was far too difficult for English forces to penetrate. A map of 1448 shows the River Dodder, now in the suburbs of Dublin, forming the southern boundary of the 'Pale'.

In 1592 you might say that an early attempt was made on the Wicklow Way, in truly horrendous conditions. Art and Henry O'Neill, and Red Hugh O'Donnell (rogues in the eyes of the English!), were imprisoned in Dublin Castle, but they broke free on a night in January. Without proper shoes or winter clothing, they headed straight for the Wicklow Mountains. Art died of exposure, while the other two reached distant Glenmalure and the protection of Fiach McHugh O'Byrne. Although this was a bitter and tragic trek, it

has occasionally been re-enacted by hardy walkers, and for the past few years the Art O'Neill Challenge has been run as a mid-winter ultra-marathon, straight through the heart of the Wicklow Mountains.

The Irish Rebellion of 1798 is remembered throughout Ireland, but it is worth particular mention with regards to the Wicklow Mountains. British forces were at a distinct disadvantage, being unable to penetrate or control the Wicklow Mountains, which in turn made it difficult to protect Dublin. In the aftermath of the rebellion, a decision was made for the military to construct a road straight through the heart of the mountains, in order to establish a series of barracks and impose authority on the area. One can only marvel at the choice of route for the Military Road, which exists in its entirety today as a signposted scenic drive. The barracks that were built at Glencree, Laragh, Drumgoff and Aghavannagh were soon decommissioned, as there was no further trouble in the area.

Of course, the turbulent politics of Ireland and Britain rumbled on, but in the Wicklow Mountains things tended to be quiet, and the landed gentry consolidated their estates. In fact, some of the landowners were highly regarded by their tenants, and sports such as grouse-shooting took place in the mountains, much as they did in Northern England and Scotland. Mining had a chequered history from 1800, lasting over 160 years.

Ireland had its Easter Rising in 1916, leading to wholesale destruction in the centre of Dublin. Although the Rising was quickly suppressed, it was quickly followed by the creation of the Irish Free State, partition of Ireland and a civil war. Land reform saw the dismantling of some large estates and the creation of a class of Irish farmers who, for the first time in centuries, owned their land.

The notion of walking for enjoyment in Ireland was often viewed as being rather odd, but the citizens of Dublin were among the first to take to the Wicklow Mountains in organised walking groups, establishing youth hostels to facilitate their explorations. JB Malone joined their ranks and eventually promoted the idea of a long-distance trail that became known as the Wicklow Way. It's now world-famous, as evidenced by the many nationalities you can expect to meet along the trail.

WILDLIFE

Ireland's more recent fossil record reveals bears, boars and the remarkable Great Irish Deer, but all are now extinct in Ireland and the only big mammals likely to be seen are domesticated cattle and sheep. Feral goats might be spotted above Glendalough, where Ireland's last wolf is claimed to have been slain. Red deer were native to the Wicklow Mountains, but have bred with the smaller, imported Sika deer over several decades, so that it is now very rare to spot a true red deer. Fallow deer are also present in small numbers.

Both foxes and hares might be spotted, albeit rarely, on the Wicklow Way. Badgers are also elusive, preferring to appear at night, and while otters are present, fishing in rivers, encounters are very rare. Extensive forests are bad for many species, though pine martens naturally flourish there. Native red and introduced grey squirrels can also be seen. The lower farmlands support plenty of rabbits, while smaller rodents such as rats and mice keep a low profile. Almost all of Ireland's bat species could be observed around the Wicklow Mountains, though this is best done at dusk, using bat detection equipment. Bats devour plenty of biting midges every summer evening!

Grouse shooting was once popular in the Wicklow Mountains, but these days only small areas are managed for the sport. Red grouse are permanent residents on the moors, able to survive the bitter winters. The cries of peregrine falcons can be heard above rocky glens such as Glendalough, as can the croak of ravens. Owls are present, though best spotted at dusk when they start hunting. Tiny wrens make their homes in rocky holes and drystone walls, and it used to be common for boys to hunt for them on 26th December.

PLANTLIFE

A famous early 19th-century Irish lament, *Caoine Cill Chais*, is a sorry story about the destruction of Ireland's last great woodlands. It begins…

> *'Cad a dhéanfaimid feasta gan adhmad?*
> *Tá deireadh na gcoillte ar lár'*
> 'What will we do now for wood?
> With the last of the woods laid low'

Ireland was once very well-wooded, and the stumps of ancient trees are commonly found wherever turf (peat) is cut for fuel. However, almost all the forests seen today are fairly recent commercial plantations, largely comprised of Sitka spruce and Douglas fir. Scots pines – which used to be native, but became extinct in Ireland thousands of years ago – have been reintroduced into some forests.

Oak trees are not only common, but have always been held in high regard as a sacred tree in Ireland. The letters of the ancient Irish alphabet were largely based on the names of trees. Yet centuries of felling, with little replanting, has left Ireland as one of the most sparsely wooded countries in Europe.

Some small, self-regenerating woodlands cling to the sides of steep and rugged glens, featuring gnarled oaks and hardy rowans, while mature woodlands at lower levels are invariably secondary plantations. A typical deciduous woodland might contain oak and birch, maybe with an understorey of hazel and holly, tangled with ivy and honeysuckle. Some of the commercial plantations might include older, hidden stands of mature beech trees.

The ancient art of crafting shillelagh sticks survives, appropriately, at Shillelagh in Co Wicklow, not far from the last remnants of one of Ireland's ancient forests, at Coolattin.

The higher slopes of the Wicklow Mountains are notable for their heather cover, though this varies according to how wet the ground is. The drier slopes often feature extensive bracken cover, while the wetter slopes might feature tussocky moor grasses and bog cotton, with tiny sundews and butterworts trapping the smallest insects. Damp, sheltered areas often support a range of ferns, mosses and liverworts. Saxifrages tend to favour areas of rock and scree, but extensive bare rock might only support patches of lichen.

While some fields low in the glens sprout good flowery grasslands, which can be mown for hay or silage, other fields will be seen sprouting little more than bracken, gorse and brambles. The most rampant vegetation is found among the hedgerows, where blackthorn and hawthorn grow, and along roadside verges. Spring and summer reveal all kinds of flowering plants growing in gloriously colourful tangles.

Some estates and country houses planted rhododendrons, which became a nuisance in some areas, while other non-native plants, such as fuchsias, flourish exceptionally well in hedgerows and gardens.

WICKLOW MOUNTAINS NATIONAL PARK

The bleak and barren crest of the Wicklow Mountains has attracted the attention of recreational walkers for over a century, but the Wicklow Mountains National Park was only designated in 1991. Some land already in state ownership was consolidated and further land holdings were acquired, so that the national park came together as a peculiar jigsaw and now covers 220km². Although some 30km of the upland crest is included, from north to south, the width of the national park varies dramatically and there are pinch points where it is less than 1km wide. Some small areas are completely detached from the main area of the park, and local farmers still own some of the grazing rights over land inside the national park. Nevertheless, much of the land is more than 500m above sea level and many major summits are included. In the future, some areas of state-owned forests adjoining the park might also be included, but two major military firing ranges on the western side of the Wicklow Mountains are completely excluded.

The Wicklow Way only passes through small areas on the eastern fringes of the national park. These include Prince William's Seat on Day 1; Djouce Mountain on Day 2; Paddock Hill on Day 3; and the ascent from Glendalough to Borenacrow on Day 4. The total distance covered by the Wicklow Way inside the national park is only 17km. Observant walkers will spot small notices announcing when the national park is being entered and when it is being left. Wild campers are permitted to pitch overnight in the national park, though not in the Glendalough valley, provided that they follow the sort of common-sense rules that experienced wild campers already follow. See Accommodation below.

The establishment of the national park wasn't without controversy. Originally, there was a plan to build a visitor centre beside a mountain road near Luggala, some 400m above sea level. This would have led to a great increase in traffic on the mountain road, as well as congestion, not to mention it being a dangerous road in mist, or when snow and ice are present. After strenuous objections were raised, the plan was abandoned. It was suggested that an appropriate location for a visitor centre would be in a nearby village, such as Roundwood, where local businesses might benefit, but that never happened. Again, at Luggala, an opportunity was missed for the state to acquire a splendid upland property that was sold as recently as 2019.

There is a small-scale national park information centre near the Upper Lake in Glendalough, beside the Wicklow Way, where some helpful maps and brochures about the national park can be obtained. Of particular interest is the leaflet *The Walking Trails of Glendalough*, which can be purchased on arrival, or downloaded for free from the national park website.

The information centre is open daily through the main summer season, or at weekends for the rest of the year, from 1000 to 1730. It may close for lunch, or whenever staff are called away. For further information, tel 0761 002667, www.wicklow mountainsnationalpark.ie.

TRAVEL TO AND FROM THE WICKLOW WAY

Nearly all walkers will travel first to Dublin, from where the start of the Wicklow Way can be accessed easily and quickly. There are many options and many timetables to juggle, but the journey is really quite easy from Britain and most parts of Europe, and even from North America (though it is unlikely that most walkers could arrive in Dublin early enough to complete a full day on the Wicklow Way). It is more likely that travel to Dublin will also involve an overnight stay in the city, making it possible to start walking early the following morning.

By air

There are plenty of airlines flying from Britain and most parts of Europe, as well as from North America, directly to Dublin Airport. The main national airline is Aer Lingus (www.aerlingus.com) and the main budget airline is Ryanair (www.ryanair.com), but there are dozens more airlines and countless routes available. On arrival at the airport, regular buses run to the centre of Dublin city, but spend a moment researching routes, as not all of them will take you where you want to go. The Airlink Express links the airport with Dublin's main railway stations. The Aircoach visits most of the major hotels in Dublin. Avoid the Airport Hopper and Airbus, as they serve outlying parts of Dublin. Dublin Bus also links the airport and city centre, but includes frequent stops. If you have no wish to stop in Dublin, then the number 16 Dublin Bus runs from the airport to the start of the Wicklow Way at Marlay Park without any need to change. Taxis are an expensive option, but are available if you wish to use them.

Views across and beyond Dublin from Kilmashogue Forest (Day 1)

By sea

Irish Ferries (www.irishferries.com) and Stena Line (www.stenaline.co.uk) both sail up to four times a day between Holyhead in North Wales and the port of Dublin, taking around 3½ hours. Most ferries are met by a coach that runs into the city centre, but check in advance if using very early or late sailings, as the coach may not run. Irish Ferries also operate thrice-weekly sailings from the French port of Cherbourg to Dublin, except during winter. Walkers based in Scotland could sail from Cairnryan to Larne or Belfast, while walkers based in South Wales could sail between Fishguard or Pembroke and Rosslare. However, using these routes would involve onward rail or bus transport to reach Dublin.

By rail

For walkers based in Ireland, Irish Rail routes converge on Dublin, while for those travelling from Britain, rail routes lead to Holyhead, Pembroke, Fishguard and Stranraer (for Cairnryan), for ferry services to Ireland. Check rail details for Britain (www.nationalrail.co.uk) and Ireland (www.irishrail.ie).

By bus

For those already in Ireland, Bus Éireann routes converge on Dublin from all parts of Ireland. The main bus station is Busáras, which is only a short walk from the city centre. Various National Express routes can be linked through Britain to reach ferry-ports serving Ireland. It is worth checking some of the links at euro lines.buseireann.ie. Megabus (www.

europebus.co.uk) offers a route from London Victoria to Pembroke, for the Irish Ferries service to Rosslare, though onward arrangements would need to be made to reach Dublin by bus or rail.

Getting to and from the route

On arrival in the centre of Dublin, reaching the start of the Wicklow Way is very easy. The best approach is to head for O'Connell Street, and in particular bus stop 270, near the junction with Cathedral Street, in order to catch the number 16 Dublin Bus directly to Marlay Park. See www.dublinbus.ie. (Change is not given on Dublin buses so it is essential to carry some small change, not banknotes, for fares.) Marlay Park is also served by the number 175 Go-Ahead bus, but this is only of any use to anyone catching it in the southern suburbs of Dublin.

Getting to and from various stages along the Wicklow Way requires very careful juggling of limited bus timetables and taxi operators. If planning to commute to and from the trail, be sure to check all available options at least a couple of days in advance to ensure that they will work for you. Dublin Bus serves Glencullen and Enniskerry, but both places are off route. The Glendalough Bus operates between Dublin, Roundwood and Glendalough. The Wicklow Way Bus operates a service linking Rathdrum with Glendalough and Glenmalure, and another service linking Rathdrum

with Iron Bridge, Tinahely and Curravanish. However, these services must be booked in advance and prices are based on at least three people travelling. Services are planned around rail services operating between Dublin and Rathdrum. Tinahely has an occasional Bus Éireann service, while Shillelagh has an occasional bus service operated by Matt Cousins. Both Tinahely and Shillelagh are served by occasional Wicklow Rural Transport services, linking with Gorey or Carlow. Taxis based at Enniskerry, Tinahely and Shillelagh are regularly used to shuttle walkers to and from the Wicklow Way.

When the time comes to leave the Wicklow Way, there are no buses serving Clonegal, at the end of the trail. It is necessary to walk for another hour or two, or organise a lift or a taxi to Kildavin or Bunclody in order to catch a bus back to Dublin. There is a direct Bus Éireann service, number 132, or use the Wexford Local Link service to link with the 132 bus from Tullow to Dublin. Be sure to check timetables well in advance at www.buseireann.ie, as the buses run at different times on different days.

WHEN TO WALK

Wicklow winters are pretty bleak, so unless you are actively looking for a difficult experience, avoid that time of year. The Wicklow Mountains get more snow and more prolonged frosts than any other part of Ireland. However, the arduous Art O'Neill Challenge takes place through the Wicklow Mountains each January, attracting particularly hardy ultra-runners.

Spring, summer and autumn can experience good weather or bad weather, and the main thing to be aware of is that the weather is bound to be changeable, even in the space of the single week that it takes to walk the trail. The sun will shine during that week, but it's also likely that it will rain at some point, and days are likely to be intermittently cloudy and clear. The only way to keep on top of the weather is by checking the weather forecast at every opportunity. The weather is rarely so bad that it would result in a day's walk having to be cancelled, but on the other hand, the prospect of trudging through rain and mist, knowing that the surrounding scenery is spectacular on a good day, might be enough to convince you to wait for better weather on the following day. Check www.met.ie or catch the weather on local news services.

Most people walk the Wicklow Way in the peak summer period, which is fine, and it will usually be warmer and drier than other times of the year. However, bear in mind that accommodation can come under pressure and it might be necessary to detour far off-route in search of accommodation, and note that popular restaurants can be so busy that it takes time to be served a meal.

ACCOMMODATION

It has to be said at the outset that there is hardly any accommodation actually on the Wicklow Way, and the mere handful of options that are on the route are found only at Knockree, Oldbridge, Glendalough and Drumgoff. Fortunately, there are other options located 1–3km off-route. Beyond this distance, it is fairly common for accommodation providers to offer a pick-up and drop-off service, and some proprietors are used to catering for Wicklow Way walkers even though they might be up to 10km off-route. However, be sure to negotiate lifts in advance, then be sure to be on time to be collected from a specific point on the trail. Not all accommodation providers offer a full meals service, so if you choose to stay in a remote place, check if it is possible to be given a lift to and from a restaurant for meals.

While much of the accommodation can be contacted direct by making phone calls, it is often possible to book through websites such as www. booking.com. It is also worth bearing in mind that some places are available through www.airbnb.com, though many of these must be booked through the website as they cannot be approached directly. Using these two websites allows properties to be located on an online map, which is really useful, and all the available facilities can be checked, as well as prices, and once bookings have been made there is a measure of protection.

Knockree Youth Hostel is close to the Wicklow Way (end of Day 1/start of Day 2)

Some walkers might approach Tourism Ireland, www.ireland.ie, to search for accommodation. This will ensure that accommodation is 'approved', but it will also mean that many accommodation options won't be mentioned, including some that are much more convenient for walkers to reach.

Be sure to inform your accommodation providers if you are going to arrive later than planned, to avoid unnecessary worry. If you need to cancel a booking, there might be penalties.

There are only two An Óige (Irish Youth Hostel Association) properties close to the Wicklow Way; one at Knockree and the other in Glendalough – see www.anoige. ie. A hostel might be used in the centre of Dublin before starting the Wicklow Way. There are a number of independent hostels in Dublin, but only a couple are located near the Wicklow Way, one near Roundwood and the other at Laragh.

Three basic wooden huts have been installed on the Wicklow Way at Brusher Gap, Mullacor and Mucklagh. These huts are in the 'Adirondack' style, having a floor, three walls and a roof, with one side being left open to the weather. They are free to use and are equipped with a picnic table and a fire pit, and as they are all in forested locations, great care has to be exercised if starting a fire. These huts are barely a step up from camping, so anyone using them would need a sleeping bag and cooking equipment. As they can't be booked and are available on a 'first come first served' basis, anyone planning on using them

The Mullacor Hut lies in the forest on the descent into Glenmalure (Day 4)

would be well advised to carry a tent, just in case they were full.

There is only one commercial campsite near the Wicklow Way, some 2.5km off-route at Roundwood. However, the Wicklow Way Lodge B&B plans to open a campsite at Oldbridge, which would actually be on the Wicklow Way. In recent years, Coillte (Irish Forestry) and the Wicklow Mountains National Park have allowed wild camping on their properties, subject to the sort of common-sense rules that dedicated wild campers already observe. For the avoidance of doubt, the following statement is taken from a notice at the start of the Wicklow Way:

'Wild camping is permitted in the Wicklow Mountains National Park and on Coillte forest properties subject to adherence to the Camping Code of Practice available from www.wicklowmountainsnationalpark.ie and www.coillte.ie.

A written permit is required:
• For groups consisting of more than ten people
• When it is proposed to light a campfire
• For all camping between 1st September and 28th February (deer hunting season)

Permits must be acquired at least seven days prior to your stay and are available from Coillte, tel 01 2011111, or the Wicklow Mountains National Park, tel 0404 45800.

Please note: Wild camping is not permitted on privately owned land, land owned by Local Authorities or in the Glendalough valley.'

FOOD AND DRINK

There are very few pubs and restaurants actually on the Wicklow Way. In fact, apart from two hotels with bars and restaurants at Glendalough and Drumgoff, as well as a pub that doesn't offer meals at Stranakelly, everything else is off-route. Short detours reveal a few more places offering food and drink, as well as the occasional shop, which are mentioned in the guidebook, but if your route plan doesn't include anything for two or three days, then be sure to stock up and carry whatever you need.

Maggie's of Tinahely claims to serve the best pint in Ireland!
(Day 6, alternative route)

MONEY MATTERS

The Euro is the currency of Ireland. Large denomination euro notes are difficult to use for small purchases, so avoid the €500 and €200 notes altogether, and the €100 notes if you can. The rest – €50, €20, €10 and €5 – are the most useful. Coins come in €2 and €1. Small denomination coins come in values of 50c, 20c, 10c, 5c, 2c and 1c. There are plenty of banks and ATMs in Dublin, but hardly any on or near the Wicklow Way. Those that are available are mentioned in the route descriptions. Some accommodation providers will accept major credit and debit cards, but please check in advance, because some of them require cash payments.

COMMUNICATIONS

There are very few payphones on or near the Wicklow Way, and there are some areas where mobile phones get little or no signal. If staying in touch is important, then be sure to monitor signal strength from time to time and make any important calls before losing the signal. Telephone numbers in this guidebook are shown with their local codes. If phoning from outside Ireland, or if using a mobile phone in Ireland, but not tied to an Irish network, first dial +353, then drop the first 0 from the phone number. Many accommodation providers offer Wi-Fi, but some don't, so be sure to check in advance if you are relying on such a service being available.

DAILY SCHEDULE

On the Wicklow Way, it's not just a case of how far you are willing to walk along the trail each day. It's also important to consider how much extra you are willing to walk in search of accommodation. Most of the stages in this guidebook end some distance from available lodgings, requiring detours off-route in the evening, and consequently back onto the route the following day. Daily distances measure from 9–23km per day, but detours off-route could add anything from 1–3km extra, unless a taxi is ordered, or a pick-up can be negotiated in advance with your accommodation provider.

Each daily stage includes an option to vary the 'official' route by switching to an adjacent waymarked trail, or some other route. Most of these options will be longer, but they will also have more scenic merit. Other options will bring extra facilities into play, or more rarely, simply offer a short-cut. Be aware of the available options each day, but also bear in mind how they affect the length of each stage, and the time needed to complete each day's walk.

The daily stages given in this guidebook are simply suggestions. There are other ways to break the trail into manageable stretches, and the route description mentions places where accommodation might be sought in the middle of a stage. Although Day 3 is the shortest stage at only 9km, it assumes that readers will be walking from Oldbridge straight to Glendalough. If accommodation can't be secured at Oldbridge, and the starting point is Roundwood, then that stage becomes 13km or even 14.5km if a diversion is also made through the village of Laragh. Of course, at the end of that stage, the fascinating Monastic City at Glendalough demands as many hours of exploration as you can spare, so the time spent on that stage could easily be as long as the time spent on a longer stage.

Generally, walkers spend about a week on the Wicklow Way, and most walkers will cover uneven distances each day while juggling accommodation options and trying not to detour too far off route to find lodgings, food and drink. If you meet others along the trail, don't be surprised to discover that they are using a completely different walking schedule to yours!

WHAT TO PACK

Most walkers will cover the Wicklow Way in the spring, summer or autumn, requiring no special winter kit. The Wicklow Way is mostly an obvious trail, with little chance of anyone getting lost, and while the weather can sometimes be cold, wet and miserable, the route is rarely far from a road and even the most remote parts are not particularly challenging, nor does the trail require the use of any special kit. Your normal hill-walking kit will be fine.

Choice of kit will depend on choosing one of three methods of completing the trail. Those who plan to be self-sufficient and camp every night will of course need a full backpacking kit, including tent, sleeping bag and cooking equipment, and they should ideally already have experience of backpacking. Those who plan to stay in hostels, hotels and B&Bs can carry much less, and the absolute basic would be: waterproofs, change of clothes, food, drink, map, compass (or GPS), torch, whistle, mobile phone and a small first-aid kit. Footwear is a personal choice, but most parts of the trail are firm and dry, so boots or walking shoes are fine. If you regularly use walking poles, then take them, but they are by no means essential. Those who wish to use baggage transfer can of course take as much as they like, knowing that the bulk of it can be transported to each overnight stop, while they walk with the lightest possible pack. See Wicklow Way Baggage, www.wicklowwaybaggage.com.

WAYMARKING AND ACCESS

In its early days, the Wicklow Way was rather sparsely marked by wooden posts that often got knocked over or simply disappeared. Signposts were rare and could easily be turned to point the wrong way. Some fools even made a campfire on a wooden footbridge and burnt a hole in it, and some wild camping spots were notoriously strewn with rubbish.

Over the years the waymarking has improved dramatically, first by using more firmly planted recycled plastic marker posts, followed by even more robust metal posts, along with increasingly detailed and secure signposting. Boggy and muddy hill paths have been largely eliminated, with substantial stretches of stout boardwalks being laid across boggy ground, along with flights of steps on steep slopes, as well as paths being surfaced with grit or gravel. Some of the recent path work has been accomplished by a voluntary organisation known as Mountain Meitheal, mountain meitheal.ie. (A *meitheal* was traditionally a gathering of people from neighbouring farms, who would help to reap each other's harvests in turn.)

Pure (Protecting Uplands and Rural Environments), www.pure project.ie, is an organisation that has helped keep the countryside clean for the past few years. 'Pure Mile' roadside signs will be noticed where local people have taken responsibility to keep at least a mile of road litter-free.

Access to lowland parts of the Wicklow Way is often restricted to tarmac roads and hard-surfaced forest tracks. This is a reflection of the access situation that was common throughout Ireland when the Wicklow Way was created. However, in recent years, the creation of additional National Looped Walks has involved farmers generously offering access in places where it was once absent. Some of these walks link with the course of the

Signposts and markers for the Wicklow Way and adjacent trails

Wicklow Way and often pass through more scenic areas, avoiding roads and forests.

The whole of the Wicklow Way and the adjacent waymarked trails should be open most of the time. However, in forested areas, there are dangers associated with timber extraction, so there will be occasional closures and detours on some forest tracks. The alternative offered on Day 2, via Lough Dan, will hopefully remain available, though it passes through an estate that was sold only in 2019. It is hoped that the new owners will continue to provide access as the previous owners did. The alternative offered on Day 5, involving an unmarked ascent of Croaghanmoira, could be unavailable at certain times due to reasons of land management or grouse shooting, in which case stay on the Wicklow Way. While dogs can be taken along the Wicklow Way, most farmers would require them to be on a leash and remain under strict control on their properties. Dogs are not allowed on Croaghanmoira.

MAPS OF THE ROUTE

In its early years, maps covering the Wicklow Way were really quite appalling, showing little useful detail, but the situation has improved dramatically over time. The following selection of maps is detailed and accurate.

The Ordnance Survey Ireland (OSI), www.osi.ie, publishes two

A splendid grassy track approaches a cottage near Lough Dan (Day 2, alternative route)

Lough Tay is seen on the descent from White Hill (Day 2)

useful scales of maps covering the Wicklow Way. The Discovery Series, at a scale of 1:50,000, covers the Wicklow Way on sheets 50, 56, 61 & 62. However, note that barely 1km of the route features on sheet 61. The OSI Adventure Series, at a scale of 1:25,000, covers most of the Wicklow Way on sheets Wicklow North, Wicklow Central and Wicklow South. However, very little of the final stage beyond Shillelagh is covered.

A fine alternative to OSI mapping is provided by EastWest Mapping, www.eastwestmapping.ie, at a scale of 1:25,000, replacing earlier 1:30,000 scale maps. There are significant overlaps between sheets, so there are sometimes options to buy one sheet or another, as follows: Dublin Mountains, Wicklow Mountains West or Wicklow East, Lugnaquilla & Glendalough and Wicklow South. However, note that coverage doesn't extend much beyond Stranakelly, between Tinahely and Shillelagh.

Harvey Maps, www.harveymaps. co.uk, produce a Wicklow Mountains map at a scale of 1:30,000. Note that this covers only three northern stages of the trail, Day 2 to Day 4, from Knockree to Glenmalure.

All the above maps are available as printed maps. All the above maps, except the OSI Adventure Series, are available as digital maps for use with GPS-enabled devices. For Ordnance Survey of Ireland and Harvey Maps, check the Viewranger app, while EastWest Mapping has its own dedicated app.

EMERGENCIES

The *gardaí* (police), ambulance, fire service or mountain rescue can be called on 999 or the European emergency number 112. There are two mountain rescue teams in Co Wicklow and both are close to the northern part of the Wicklow Way. The Dublin and Wicklow team is based at Roundwood, and the Glen of Imaal team is based at Laragh. There are no hospitals or health centres on the Wicklow Way and pharmacies are only available in nearby towns.

USING THIS GUIDE

An information box at the beginning of each daily stage provides the essential facts for the day's walk: start and finish points (including grid refs), distance covered, an estimation of time, ascent and descent figures, an overview of the types of terrain you'll encounter, relevant map sheets, and places en route (as well as slightly off-route) where you can buy refreshments and find accommodation.

Stage maps are provided at a scale of 1:50,000. In the route description, significant places or features along the way that also appear on the map extracts are highlighted in bold to aid navigation. As well as the route being described in detail, background information about places of interest is provided in brief.

Appendix A lists accommodation options along the route and, where necessary, options off-route. Appendix B provides contact details that may be useful in planning and enjoying a successful walk. Appendix C lists some Irish words frequently encountered in local place names, along with their anglicised forms and meaning in English.

GPX files

GPX tracks for the routes in this guidebook are available to download free at www.cicerone.co.uk/1050/GPX. A GPS device is an excellent aid to navigation, but you should also carry a map and compass and know how to use them. GPX files are provided in good faith, but neither the author nor the publisher accepts responsibility for their accuracy.

THE WICKLOW WAY

A glimpse of the Upper Lake in Glendalough from extensively forested slopes (Day 4)

DAY 1

Marlay Park to Knockree

Start	Marlay Park, Dublin, grid ref O 155 267
Finish	Knockree Youth Hostel, grid ref O 192 150
Distance	20km (12½ miles)
Total ascent	650m (2130ft)
Total descent	570m (1870ft)
Time	6hr 30min
Terrain	Easy road-walking and forest tracks, with short stretches of more rugged moorland paths
Maps	OSI Discovery 50 & 56, OSI Adventure Wicklow North, EastWest Dublin Mountains
Refreshments	Cafés in Marlay Park, café and pub off-route at Glencullen
Accommodation	Plenty of choice around Dublin. Knockree Youth Hostel. Next nearest options lie off-route at Enniskerry.

The Wicklow Way leaves the southern suburbs of Dublin, passing through Marlay Park. Roads and forest tracks lead into the Dublin Mountains, where there is an option to vary the route using the Dublin Mountains Way. After crossing Glencullen and the shoulder of Prince William's Seat, the route passes close to Knockree Youth Hostel above Glencree.

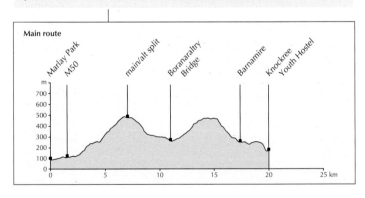

MARLAY PARK

Marlay House is the centrepiece of the extensive Marlay Park

Marlay Park is reached by catching the number 16 Dublin Bus from the centre of Dublin, or the number 175 Go-Ahead bus that runs through the southern suburbs of the city. There are bus stops near the park entrance on Grange Road. The park is based on an 18th-century demesne that has changed hands many times. The Georgian **Marlay House** is flanked by extensive lawns, the Craft Courtyard, a walled garden and belts of mature woodland. There are also numerous sports pitches. The Little Dargle River was transformed into ornamental lakes linked by small cascades. A café stands at the entrance to the walled garden, and another café is located near the exit from the park. Public access is limited to daylight hours and there might be access restrictions when music festivals take place on the extensive greens. For more information contact the park rangers, tel 086 605 6634, or visit www.dlrcoco. ie/en/parks-outdoors/parks/marlay-park.

Starting on Grange Road, walk into **Marlay Park**, keeping left of **Marlay House** to enter a car park. Look for a granite wall carved with 'The Wicklow Way' beside a map-board illustrating the route. Cross a stone step-stile and follow a tarmac path straight through a grassy area. A marker post stands at a junction of five tarmac paths, where one path leads straight ahead and slightly downhill into woodland. ▶ The **Little Dargle River** lies to the

The woodland is mature and mixed, with tall trees and a holly understorey.

left, spanned by a stone footbridge, but avoid it and keep straight ahead, then keep straight ahead again, avoiding a concrete bridge.

Later, turn left as marked to cross a wide bridge between two ponds, then turn right at a path intersection, as signposted for College Road. Keep straight ahead until the tarmac path reaches two footbridges beside a tiny waterfall. Cross either of the bridges and turn left along a gravel path. This eventually reaches a junction with a broad tarmac path. Turn right as signposted for College Road, passing fitness equipment. Note a white building on the right, which is the Wicklow Way Café, and the last refreshment opportunity until distant Glencullen, which is itself off-route. Walk straight through a car park and turn left to leave Marlay Park.

Turn right along College Road, which runs parallel to the busy M50 motorway. ◄ Turn left as signposted at a road junction and pass beneath the motorway, then turn left at a roundabout and walk up Kilmashogue Lane. Pass the entrances to St Columba's College and Ballynascorney Golf Club, and the lane climbs past a number of houses, including the thatched Fál Mór. Keep climbing until a left turn leads into the Kilmashogue Forest Recreation Area.

Follow the track to the right of a car park. ◄ Fork left at a track junction and pass a noticeboard about **Kilmashogue Forest**. The track climbs gently and eventually features a couple of prominent bends. To the left is a clear-felled and replanted slope, overlooking the sprawl of Dublin, the plains, and the coastline from the Hill of Howth to the Cooley Hills and Mountains of Mourne. Keep climbing, but watch for a marker post indicating a right turn up a few chunky granite steps, and leave the track at that point.

A path climbs, with forest to the left and a valley and a few houses down to the right. Open moorland lies ahead, featuring heather, gorse, bilberry, rushes, grass and tiny flowers. Cross a gentle crest around 490m, losing sight of Dublin behind, but facing the rolling Wicklow Mountains ahead. Reach a marked junction where the Wicklow Way joins the Dublin Mountains Way, where an

Watch for three 'fake' trees that are actually mobile phone masts.

A vague path uphill on the right offers a detour to a tumbled Megalithic tomb.

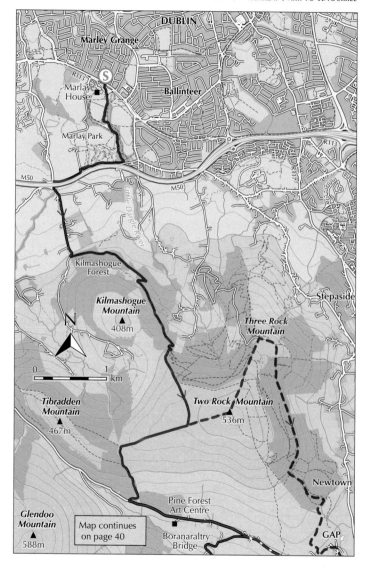

DUBLIN

Marley Grange

R113

Ⓢ Marlay House

Ballinteer

Marlay Park

M50

M50

R113

Little Dargle River

Kilmashogue Forest

Stepaside

Kilmashogue Mountain ▲ 408m

Three Rock Mountain

N

0 — 1 km

Two Rock Mountain ▲ 536m

Tibradden Mountain ▲ 467m

Newtown

Glendoo Mountain ▲ 588m

Map continues on page 40

Pine Forest Art Centre

Boranaraltry Bridge

GAP

37

alternative route is available. Turn left for the alternative route, or turn right to continue along the Wicklow Way. Both routes re-join at Boranaraltry Lane in Glencullen,

Alternative via the Dublin Mountains Way
Additional 4km (2½ miles), 70m (230ft) ascent/descent, 1hr 15min

There are two benefits to following this alternative. One is that it climbs to a fine viewpoint on Two Rock Mountain. The other is that it visits Glencullen village, which offers a café, pub, accommodation and occasional bus services.

Turn left to follow an obvious, well-trodden path straight uphill, quickly reaching the summit of **Two Rock Mountain**, crowned by a large Bronze Age cairn known as Fairy Castle, and a trig point at 536m. Views embrace the Wicklow Mountains, Dún Laoghaire, Dublin and the coastline from the Hill of Howth to the Cooley Hills and Mountains of Mourne.

A wooden walkway surrounds the summit and three main paths leave it. Be sure to follow the path heading roughly northwards, down towards Dublin. It is rugged at first, but becomes gritty and boulder-paved, running between a moorland slope and a forest. Land on a track and keep straight ahead, then turn right at a crossroads on **Three Rock Mountain**, around 430m. Follow a broad

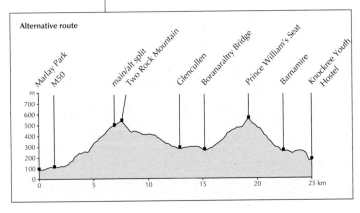

Alternative route

track while noting three granite tors and an assortment of ugly communication masts. This area is usually busy with visitors.

An obvious path along a moorland crest high above Glencullen

The track descends from a moorland slope into a forest, passing a barrier and always keeping straight ahead at any junctions. Trees obscure views, except for one stretch overlooking the urban sprawl of Dún Laoghaire. Watch out on the left for a path – definitely not the one where entry is forbidden – but the one shortly after it. Go through a small gate in a fence and observe all the safety notices that are displayed, taking care each time the forest path crosses mountain bike paths. The path later runs beside a fenced track then passes through the forest again.

Emerge from the forest to cross a metal mesh footbridge then follow a gravel path as it winds downhill, often with a mountain bike path running parallel. Later, the path passes the **GAP** (Glencullen Adventure Park) café. Turn right to walk through a car park and follow an access road through a grassy area to link with a road. Turn left to visit Johnnie Fox's pub in **Glencullen** village. ▶ The number 44B Dublin offers an infrequent, weekday-only link to Dundrum in Dublin city.

Johnnie Fox's claims to be the highest pub in Ireland. This isn't true, but it does offer food, drink and a quirky little museum.

39

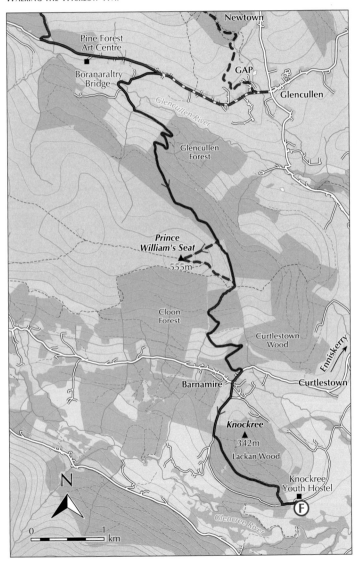

Johnnie Fox's pub at Glencullen abounds in antiques

If not visiting Glencullen village, turn right along the road, passing the Gaelic Athletic Association (GAA) Stars of Erin ground and a Christmas tree farm. ▸ The road eventually reaches a Wicklow Way signpost at a road junction, where you re-join the main route and a left turn leads down Boranaraltry Lane.

The main GAA sports are Gaelic football and hurling, played at local, county, provincial and all-Ireland levels.

Main route
Turning right, the Wicklow Way and Dublin Mountains Way follow the same pulverised granite path down a rugged moorland crest. The path has stones and boulders embedded in it, and a number of puddles after rain. The path swings left to descend beside a forest, where the Dublin Mountains Way turns right to enter the forest on **Tibradden Mountain**, and the Wicklow Way simply continues straight downhill. The Wicklow Way later enters the forest and passes a redundant gate before a short, steep descent lands suddenly on a road in Glencullen.

Turn left and follow the road as signposted. Note an access road on the right for the **Pine Forest Art Centre**, which offers educational art and craft courses for young people. However, keep straight ahead along the road and later note the 'Perfect Irish Gift' on the left, where people

This is where the alternative route joins with the main route.

are invited to purchase a square foot or more of land. A signposted road junction is reached. ◄ A right turn leads down Boranaraltry Lane.

Houses on the way down the lane generally have their names carved on big blocks of granite. The road swings left to cross **Boranaraltry Bridge**, where prominent dates in its history are carved into stone on the parapets. Walk straight ahead as marked at a junction, rising to gates where the road gives way to a gravel track. Enjoy views over Glencullen until a gate gives access to **Glencullen Forest**, and shortly after entering, turn right as marked up another forest track. The track is quite bendy as it climbs and there is a junction on one bend. Turn left, in effect keeping straight ahead, following a track to the edge of the forest. A path continues onto a heathery moor dotted with stray spruce trees, then note that a short extension is possible, though it is best reserved for use in clear, dry conditions.

Extension onto Prince William's Seat
Additional 1km (½ mile), 85m (280ft) ascent/descent, 30min
On leaving the forest, turn right, then quickly turn left just after a solitary tree and just before a small Wicklow Mountains National Park marker post. There is a path, but

A short detour can include the summit of Prince William's Seat

it is rather vague at first, then it becomes much more obvious as it climbs a boggy, heathery slope. There is no mistaking the path, which leads straight to the summit of **Prince William's Seat**, crowned by a huddle of granite boulders and a trig point at 555m. You can retrace your steps, or else turn sharp left to follow another path downhill, which leads back to the Wicklow Way. Turn right to continue.

Follow the path across the moorland slope, passing deep heather while catching glimpses between the spruce trees of the Hill of Howth, Bray and the Great Sugar Loaf. The path becomes crudely boulder-paved as it descends through young forest, and some of the boulders wobble underfoot. An easier path continues down to a forest track. Turn left down the track, passing through clear-felled and replanted areas where there are views across Glencree. Further down the bendy track, pass tall, straight Scots pines in **Curtlestown Wood**, then soon afterwards pass a barrier at a parking area to reach a road. ▶

If a taxi pick-up can be organised, it is 4.5km left along the road to Enniskerry.

Turn right as signposted along the road, then turn left at a junction beside a few houses. The road rises a little, then after turning right at a junction at **Barnamire**, it descends. A forest track on the left is signposted and flanked by two tall pines. Take the track, which rises across the slopes of **Knockree**, then once it descends gently, only the Great Sugar Loaf is seen ahead. Note a bench on the left, then turn right down a grassy path, passing another bench. Drop more steeply down a narrower path, passing a ladder stile before landing on a road. The Wicklow Way heads to the right, but anyone intending to break their journey here should turn left. A short walk leads to **Knockree Youth Hostel**. ▶

If staying off-route at Enniskerry, a taxi pick-up can be organised here.

The old 18th-century building still exists at **Knockree Youth Hostel**, which accommodated hostellers from as early as 1938, as well as housing a family and a small shop. The modern hostel dates from 2008 and offers a lot more space and facilities. The dining room offers a splendid view across Glencree to the shapely peak of the Great Sugar Loaf.

The prominent Great Sugar Loaf as seen from Knockree Youth Hostel

ENNISKERRY AND POWERSCOURT

Local taxis are accustomed to providing pick-ups and drop-offs between the Wicklow Way and the attractive village of Enniskerry. Walkers who want hotel or B&B accommodation, shop, pubs and restaurants tend to favour heading there, but it lies 5.5km off-route. The village was built to house workers on the extensive **Powerscourt Estate**. There is an entry charge to visit the estate, tel 01 204 6000, www.powerscourt.com. Note that there is no direct access to the estate from the Wicklow Way, and a proper exploration would take a whole day. **Powerscourt Waterfall** can be seen to good effect, free of charge, on Day 2 of the Wicklow Way.

Enniskerry is served by the number 44 Dublin Bus, while local services are provided by number 185 Go-Ahead buses. Being so close to Dublin, Dún Laoghaire and Bray, there are plenty of taxi operators, but Kevin, on 087 257 2973, does most of the pick-ups and drop-offs for Wicklow Way walkers.

DAY 2

Knockree to Oldbridge

Start	Knockree Youth Hostel, grid ref O 192 150
Finish	Wicklow Way Lodge, Oldbridge, grid ref O 156 014
Distance	21km (13 miles)
Total ascent	720m (2360ft)
Total descent	650m (2130ft)
Time	6hr 30min
Terrain	Forest paths and tracks, as well as exposed hill paths with little shelter. A choice between forest tracks or valley paths towards the end.
Maps	OSI Discovery 56, OSI Adventure Wicklow North and Wicklow Central, EastWest Wicklow East
Refreshments	None on the route, plenty of choice off-route at Roundwood
Accommodation	B&B at Oldbridge, other options off-route at Roundwood, or on the alternative route near Lough Dan

The Wicklow Way reaches its highest point on the shoulder of Djouce Mountain, and on a clear day a summit bid is recommended. The higher parts of the route are inside the Wicklow Mountains National Park. On reaching the Pier Gates above Luggala, a splendid alternative route could be enjoyed, taking in the scenic Lough Dan in preference to the main route. Roundwood village lies off-route, in an area where there are otherwise very few useful facilities.

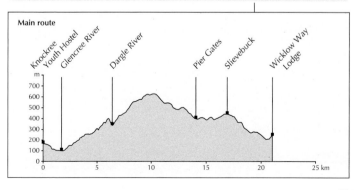

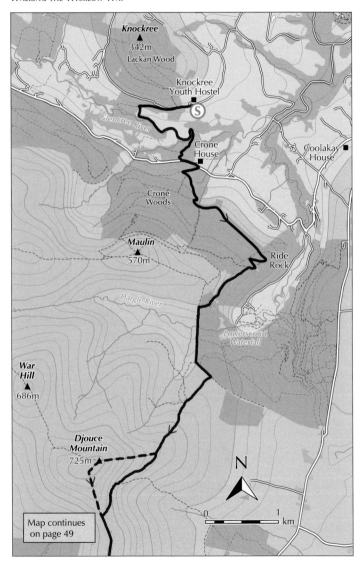

Knockree
342m
Lackan Wood

Knockree
Youth Hostel

Glencree River

Crone
House

Coolakay
House

Crone
Woods

Maulin
570m

Ride
Rock

Dargle River

Powerscourt
Waterfall

War
Hill
686m

Djouce
Mountain
725m

N

0   1
km

Map continues
on page 49

Leave Knockree Youth Hostel by following the road back to where the Wicklow Way crosses it, and keep left at a parking space as signposted. Walk down a gentle forest path, later turning left as marked down through a kissing gate. Leave the forest, walk straight down to the wooded banks of the **Glencree River** and turn left to follow it downstream. ▸ Pass grassy and bracken-clad areas, then cross a footbridge and pass a plantation of Scots pines. Follow a path uphill and turn right up a forest track, passing a clear-felled slope. The bendy track rises to a barrier and a road. Turn left along the road and pass **Crone House**.

Mixed woodland along the riverbanks include plenty of alder.

Turn right as signposted into a car park for the Crone Forest Recreation Area, often referred to as **Crone Woods**. ▸ Walk up a forest track and turn left at a junction and map-board. Climb further and the track bends right, reaching another junction. Turn left and keep climbing, levelling out on a replanted slope with views of Glencree and the Great Sugar Loaf. Enter a mature beech and pine forest, later leaving it to follow the track as it rises through replanted forest.

Note that Coolakay House B&B is signposted 3km off-route.

The track bends as it climbs, reaching a 'surprise' viewpoint at **Ride Rock**, around 260m, taking in the milky cascade of Powerscourt Waterfall and Djouce Mountain.

A view of the Powerscourt Waterfall from Ride Rock

A bench lies a little further uphill and the schist bedrock pokes through worn parts of the path. Pass another bench and enjoy the view, before it is obscured by forest. Keep climbing and the path eventually regains views as the trees become shorter and sparser. Go through a gap in a fence and a tumbled wall then turn left to drop down a steep, boulder-paved path to cross a footbridge spanning the **Dargle River**. Nearby slopes are covered in heather, gorse and bracken.

Climb alongside a tumbled wall, crossing it at a stone step-stile on the left, beside a gate. Continue uphill until a path junction is reached and another stone step-stile can be crossed on the right. A clear and obvious stony path rises on heather and bilberry slopes. The path later becomes pleasantly grassy and views open up well as height is gained. When a path junction and a marker post are reached, there is an option to continue straight ahead along the Wicklow Way, or turn right to climb Djouce Mountain.

Extension over Djouce Mountain
Additional 0.5km (⅓ mile), 170m (560ft) ascent/descent, 15min
Turn right and follow a broad and well-trodden path straight uphill, passing a couple of fenced enclosures protecting areas that suffered erosion. The path leads straight to the summit of **Djouce Mountain**, where a trig point stands at 725m on a slightly overhanging outcrop of schist.

> **Djouce Mountain** is the highest point that can be reached without detouring too far from the Wicklow Way. Views take in most of the Wicklow Mountains from Kippure to Croaghanmoira, with a glimpse of the central plains through the Sally Gap. The Great Sugar Loaf and Vartry reservoirs are also in view, while beyond the Hill of Howth, it might be possible to spot the Cooley Hills and Mountains of Mourne. On days of exceptional clarity, it will be possible to see Snowdonia in North Wales.

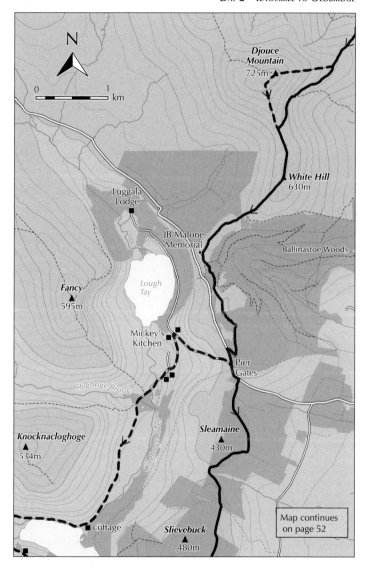

N

0   1
km

Djouce Mountain
725m

White Hill
630m

Luggala Lodge

JB Malone Memorial

Ballinastoe Woods

Fancy
595m

Lough Tay

Mickey's Kitchen

Pier Gates

Cloghoge Brook

Sleamaine
430m

Knocknacloghoge
534m

Cloghoge River

cottage

Slievebuck
480m

Map continues on page 52

49

JB Malone's memorial lies under a granite boulder above Lough Tay

Keep slightly left while passing the summit to pick up and follow a broad and stony path, which drops to a corner on a prominent boardwalk where the Wicklow Way is re-joined. Keep straight ahead and follow the boardwalk path.

If not intending to climb Djouce Mountain, simply keep straight ahead and follow the Wicklow Way across the eastern flank of the mountain, gradually rising along a narrow but obvious path. A boardwalk path is joined and followed, soon turning left along a broad crest.

Cross a gentle dip and simply let the boardwalk path lead the way over the broad and boggy top of **White Hill**, at 630m. ◄ Bog cotton is spotted and water fills bog-holes, but feet remain dry while following the boardwalk path. There is a break in the boardwalk where you cross firm ground on a gentle gap, with forest nearby. Pass a redundant stile and follow another long stretch of the boardwalk path along a high crest.

Pass a memorial, apparently commemorating the late Tom Walsh's boots! Soon afterwards, there is a short break in the boardwalk where quartz-rich rock is exposed. Thirty steps lead down to a viewing platform on the right,

For those who didn't climb Djouce Mountain, this is the highest point on the Wicklow Way.

where the **JB Malone memorial** is tucked beneath a huge granite boulder. ▶ There are splendid views across Lough Tay to the higher Wicklow Mountains.

JB Malone conceived the Wicklow Way and steered it into being.

Another 100 steps lead downhill and it is important to keep left at a boardwalk path junction, soon passing a map-board and continuing along a forest path. The path later crosses a forest track, continuing on the other side, climbing a slope. A viewpoint lies just to the right, otherwise keep straight ahead, later noting another viewpoint just to the left in a clear-felled and replanted forest. Mature forest is entered and another stretch of boardwalk path drops gently with the aid of 164 widely spaced steps. Turn right at the end and follow a path through dense, dark forest to emerge on a mountain road. Turn left and walk down the road to reach the Pier Gates, where a choice needs to be made between the main Wicklow Way and an alternative route.

Alternative via Lough Dan
Additional 3km (2 miles), 50m (165ft) ascent/descent, 1hr
This alternative route is splendid and scenic, but it shouldn't be used if there is any risk that rivers will be swollen, as one river needs to be forded. Walkers who intend moving off-route to Roundwood should stay on the main route. Access has been allowed on this alternative

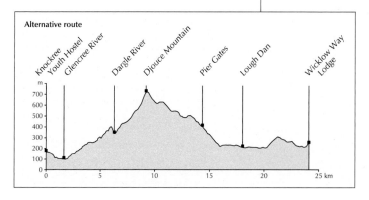

Alternative route

Knockree Youth Hostel · Glencree River · Dargle River · Djouce Mountain · Pier Gates · Lough Dan · Wicklow Way Lodge

m
700
600
500
400
300
200
100
0

0   5   10   15   20   25 km

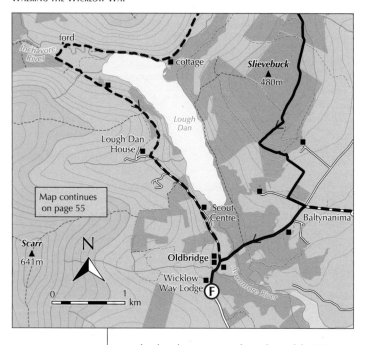

route for decades, courtesy of members of the Guinness family, who owned the estate. However, the estate was sold in 2019, so it is hoped that access will continue to be available. Check luggala.com for news of restrictions.

The prominent Pier Gates stand beside a smaller kissing gate and a notice says that the gates will be locked at 5.30pm. Go through the kissing gate and follow a narrow road down to a couple of cottages, one of which is known as **Mickey's Kitchen**. Turn left to continue descending, noting that there is no access to the right to Lough Tay. ◄ Another stout set of gates are reached and if these are closed, use a stone step-stile beside them. Go straight down through a crossroads as signposted and the road becomes a track, soon crossing a wooden bridge over the **Cloghoge River**, followed by another wooden bridge over the **Cloghoge Brook**.

Luggala Lodge can't be seen, but it is like a miniature white-painted castle.

Cross a stile beside a gate and continue along a track that is often delightfully grassy, flanked by walls, sometimes on both sides, sometimes on one side or neither side, as it undulates gently alongside a fine valley grazed by sheep and deer. Keep right of a little white cottage and the grassy path becomes enclosed by dense gorse bushes beside **Lough Dan**. Stay on the most obvious well-trodden path but expect to receive a few scratches along the way.

Emerging from the gorse bushes at the head of the lake, there is rocky and boggy ground ahead, but there are a couple of well-trodden paths available. Aim to keep clear of the wettest parts, but also keep an eye on the convoluted course of the **Inchavore River**. The river is often very deep and after a spell of rain it can also flow fast and prove dangerous to ford. The **ford** should be obvious, exploiting a stony shoal where the water is shallow, and there might well be stepping stones that allow the river to be crossed dry-shod. ▶

Step up from the river and walk straight across a broad, level, grassy area, aiming towards two huge, flat-topped granite boulders close to a forest. Turn left to

If the river is in flood, an inconvenient detour must be made further upstream to find a safe crossing. Don't cross if it seems unsafe, but retreat to the Pier Gates.

A crucial ford needs to be located on the Inchavore River

follow a level grassy track, joining a stony track beside some ruined houses. Climb from the valley along a stony track, passing high above **Lough Dan**, with forest occasionally obscuring lake views. Pass a little house and go through a gate while following the track, then watch carefully to spot a path dropping to the left to a kissing gate.

Go through the kissing gate and a scenic path passes a granite memorial bench to Ronnie Petrie, who provided the access here. The path later runs into woodland, then a little gate leads onto a road. ◄ Turn left down the road and cross a bridge then the road undulates with occasional glimpses of Lough Dan. Pass a **Scout Centre** to reach a signposted crossroads at **Oldbridge**. Turn right uphill to reach the **Wicklow Way Lodge B&B**.

Lough Dan House B&B lies up this road.

Main route
Leave the Pier Gates and follow the road round a bend, then turn right as signposted along a forest track. ◄ Always stay on the most obvious track, winding and undulating around the slopes of **Sleamaine**, with views from clear-felled and replanted areas, taking in either mountains or reservoirs. Roundwood village will be noticed down to the left, but a track leading down towards it is clearly marked as private. Stay on the forest track as marked and signposted, rising across the slopes of **Slievebuck**.

The road can be used to reach accommodation further downhill, in the direction of Roundwood.

On one descent, watch out for a marker post pointing to the right, up a path through a young part of the forest. Take this path, following it up and down, catching a glimpse of Lough Dan, and land on a track. Turn left up the track, then follow it down into a dip, turning right as marked down a grassy path into dense, dark forest. Emerge to cross a ladder stile and walk down beside a field to reach an arrangement of gates. Turn right to cross a ladder stile and walk beside another field, going through a kissing gate to follow an enclosed path to another ladder stile, reaching a track. Turn left up the track to reach a signposted crossroads at **Baltynanima** and consider two options.

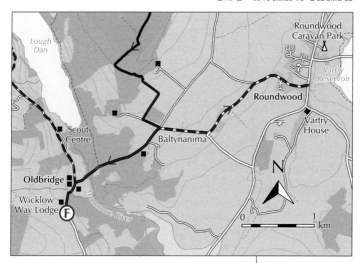

The Wicklow Way turns right, while the village of **Roundwood** lies straight ahead. Turning right and following the road downhill leads through a splendid mature oak-wood. Notices illustrate the natural history of the woodland. A bridge spans the **Avonmore River** to reach **Oldbridge**, where there is a crossroads. Simply walk straight ahead as signposted, up to the **Wicklow Way Lodge B&B**. ▶

This is one of the few B&Bs actually on the route, and it is planning to operate a campsite too. The proprietors offer plenty of information about local walking opportunities.

Off-route to Roundwood
2.5km (1½ miles), 60m (195ft) descent, 45min
From the crossroads at Baltynanima, Roundwood is signposted straight ahead. The road is later signposted left at one junction and right at another, entering **Roundwood** at a junction beside The Roundwood Inn and The Coach House. The village offers accommodation, including a **campsite**, pubs, restaurants, shops, ATM and post office. **Vartry House** claims to be the highest pub in Ireland, but it isn't. St Kevin's Bus links the village with Dublin and Glendalough, while Local Link 183 buses connect the village with Wicklow and Glendalough.

DAY 3
Oldbridge to Glendalough

Start	Wicklow Way Lodge, Oldbridge, grid ref O 156 014
Finish	Glendalough Hotel, grid ref T 124 969
Distance	9km (5½ miles)
Total ascent	300m (985ft)
Total descent	400m (1310ft)
Time	3hr
Terrain	Mostly easy road-walking, forest tracks and paths, with a few short ascents and descents
Maps	OSI Discovery 56, OS Adventure Wicklow Central, EastWest Wicklow Mountains West or Lugnaquilla & Glendalough.
Refreshments	Roundwood (off-route), Laragh (off-route), Glendalough Hotel
Accommodation	Roundwood (off-route), Oldbridge, Brusher Gap Hut, Laragh (off-route), Glendalough

This might seem like a short day's walk, but if you start off-route at Roundwood, there is just over 4km of road-walking needed to reach Oldbridge, where the route description starts. Also, after crossing Paddock Hill, there is an option to detour through the village of Laragh, which offers a range of useful services, but adds another 1.5km. At the end of the day, the ancient Monastic City at Glendalough demands at least an hour's exploration, or longer if the nearby visitor centre is also included.

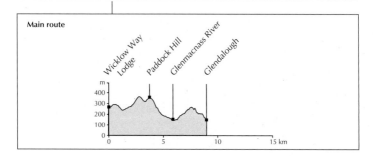

56

Leave the Wicklow Way Lodge at Oldbridge by walking up a steep road, which soon levels out, with fields rising to the right and a wooded slope dropping to the left. The road descends to cross a little river, then climbs and passes a few houses. Turn right as signposted up a track, and note that a **farmhouse** later offers a water tap for passing walkers. Cross a step-stile beside a gate and walk up the track to cross another step-stile beside another gate at Brusher Gap. Turn left to cross yet another step-stile and follow a path uphill beside a forest. Look back to spot Scarr, Djouce Mountain and the Great Sugar Loaf. The path enters the forest and descends gently, then there are fields to the left and the **Brusher Gap Hut** is seen to the right.

Fields are passed on the way from Roundwood to Oldbridge

> The **Brusher Gap Hut** is one of three open shelters on the Wicklow Way. They are built in the 'Adirondack' style, which originated in the forests of upstate New York. They are built with three wooden walls, a roof and a floor, with one side left completely open. A picnic table and a fire ring are available outside.

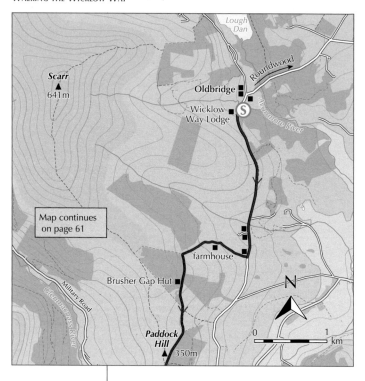

Look back to see the
Great Sugar Loaf.

Continue down the path, leaving the edge of the forest by crossing a step-stile over a fence. Cross a slope of
bracken to reach a distant marker post and turn right to
walk gently uphill beside another forest. ◄ Bracken gives
way to heather on the shoulder of **Paddock Hill**, around
350m, then there is more bracken as the path descends.
Turn right as directed by a marker post and follow a
broad, grassy path steeply downhill. Cross a step-stile
over a forest fence and immediately turn right.

A path runs along the top side of the forest then
descends through it. Note that there are a number of
other paths intersecting, so always be guided by the
marker posts and stay on the most well-trodden path. Pass

Walkers descend a steepening path from Paddock Hill

through an oak-wood before joining a track, then turn right to follow the track to a barrier gate and the **Military Road** in Glenmacnass. Cross over the road to find a noticeboard and a woodland path. The path incorporates a number of surfaces and was built to demonstrate how different methods of construction suit different types of ground conditions. When a stretch of boardwalk path leads to a junction, there is a choice of routes, depending on whether you want (or need) to visit the nearby village of Laragh, or stay on the main route.

Diversion through Laragh
Extra 1.5km (1 mile), 50m (165ft) ascent/descent, 30min
Turn left at the path junction and climb quickly back to the **Military Road** then turn right to follow it. The road leads past Glendalough Glamping to reach a junction at Glendalough Green, where there is a grocery shop and café. Turn right to follow the road across the Avonmore River to enter the village of **Laragh**. At this point, you can either turn left or turn right at a junction.

Turning left at the junction leads to Lynams of Laragh, offering hotel accommodation, food and drink, with the Wicklow Way Hostel just beyond. A couple more B&Bs lie further along the road. Keeping right at the junction, however, leads past McCoy's Convenience Store

Glendalough Green and the village of Laragh lie a short way off-route

and the Wicklow Heather restaurant, which also offers accommodation.

Turn right as signposted for the Outdoor Store and follow the road up past **St Kevin's Church** and school. Keep just to the left of the Pinewood B&B to follow a track that eventually passes a house, followed by a barrier gate, to enter a forest. When a track intersection is reached in **Brockagh Forest**, turn left to re-join the Wicklow Way.

Alternative route

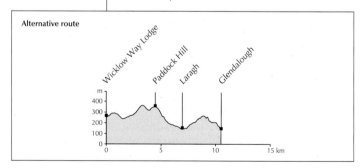

60

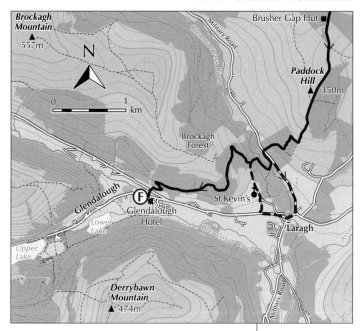

Main route

Turn right at the junction and cross a footbridge over the boulder-bedded **Glenmacnass River**. The path climbs and turns right among tall pines, with a deciduous understorey and a dense ground cover of bilberries. The path leads to a track, where a right turn leads to an intersection of tracks in **Brockagh Forest**. The diversion through Laragh joins here and the Wicklow Way runs straight ahead. ▸

It is still possible to turn left to visit Laragh, returning the same way to continue.

The track climbs into younger forest and after turning left at a junction, there are masses of gorse bushes alongside. The track reaches a turning space, where a path continues, reaching a redundant step-stile followed by taller forest for a short stretch. The path is worn to schist bedrock as it climbs past gorse bushes, catching a brief glimpse of Glendalough and its two lakes. After heading back into tall forest, the path descends steeply, becoming narrower before levelling out.

The forest is mixed, but has some notable Scots pine trees. Watch for a marker post indicating a sharp left turn downhill. The pines give way to beeches just as a step-stile is reached. Walk down a grassy, bushy slope to find another step-stile and a signposted road crossing. A final short path leads straight down to another road in front of the **Glendalough Hotel**. At this point there are a number of options to consider.

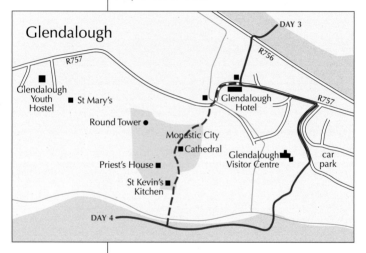

Glendalough, or *Gleann Dá Loch*, is the Valley of the Two Lakes. The Glendalough Hotel is the obvious place to eat, drink and stay, though the road can be followed to the right, across a bridge and onwards, for an overnight at the modernised Glendalough Youth Hostel. Just behind the hotel, across the bridge, is a stone arch giving access to the immensely popular Monastic City. Alternatively, turn left away from the hotel, then turn right for the Glendalough Visitor Centre, in order to learn about the significance of the monastic site before exploring it.

The Glendalough Youth Hostel lies a little off the Wicklow Way.

THE MONASTIC CITY

A small rural monastery was founded in Glendalough in the 7th century and it grew until it was eclipsed by the founding of larger Norman monasteries in the 13th century. At its peak, the monastery was a renowned centre of learning. The Glendalough Visitor Centre, tel 0404 45325 or 45352, offers plenty of information about rural Irish monasteries, and guides are available to lead visitors through the site. Notice how the stonework is mostly schist, rather than granite.

The most popular features are the tall **Round Tower** and a curious church known as **St Kevin's Kitchen**, which has a miniature round tower poking from its roof. A ruined **Cathedral** dedicated to St Peter and St Paul was built in several stages and was once quite ornate. It ceased to be a cathedral in 1214. Nearby is the monolithic **St Kevin's Cross**, which might be the oldest monument on the site, sculpted between the 6th and 8th centuries. Some say that St Kevin was buried beneath it. The nearby 12th-century **Priest's House** might have held relics of the saint. The **Gatehouse**, which is near the Glendalough Hotel, was built in the 10th or 11th century. Collectively, the ruins and other nearby sites are known as the **Seven Churches**, and a whole day might be spent making a leisurely tour around them. It used to be said that seven pilgrimages to Glendalough were equal to one pilgrimage to Rome, but after a series of pilgrimages ended with drunken brawls, faction fights and riots, they were banned altogether in the 19th century.

St Kevin's Kitchen is a curious ancient church in Glendalough

St Kevin

St Kevin lived as a hermit in Glendalough in the 6th century. According to tradition, he inhabited a cave known as St Kevin's Bed above the Upper Lake. In order to mortify his flesh, he waded into the cold waters of the lake and raised his hands in prayer. They say he prayed so fervently that he didn't notice a bird building a nest in his outstretched palm. Being a gentle man, he waited until the eggs were hatched and the fledglings had flown before leaving the lake. Of such men are legends born and Glendalough duly became a place of pilgrimage.

St Kevin's Way

A waymarked pilgrim trail called St Kevin's Way crosses the Wicklow Mountains from Hollywood or Valleymount to finish at Glendalough. From either of the two starting points, the route mostly follows quiet roads then switches to forest tracks to approach the scenic Wicklow Gap. Descending from the gap, the route links with the Miners' Way in Glendasan to reach Glendalough. The trail measures 30km.

DAY 4
Glendalough to Glenmalure

Start	Glendalough Hotel, grid ref T 124 969
Finish	Glenmalure Lodge, Drumgoff, grid ref T 106 908
Distance	14km (8¾ miles)
Total ascent	460m (1510ft)
Total descent	460m (1510ft)
Time	4hr 30min
Terrain	Mostly along forest tracks and an upland boardwalk, with the alternative route using a valley track, mountain paths and a boardwalk.
Maps	OSI Discovery 56, OS Adventure Wicklow Central, EastWest Lugnaquilla & Glendalough
Refreshments	Glendalough and Glenmalure
Accommodation	Glendalough, Mullacor Hut and Glenmalure

Soon after starting this day's walk, two very different alternatives are available. The Wicklow Way is largely confined to forest as it climbs from Glendalough onto the broad upland gap of Borenacrow. An alternative route is available along the Miners' Way, which is only a little longer but significantly more scenic, provided that the weather is good. Both routes re-join at Borenacrow to descend through forest into Glenmalure.

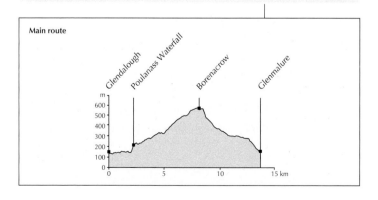

65

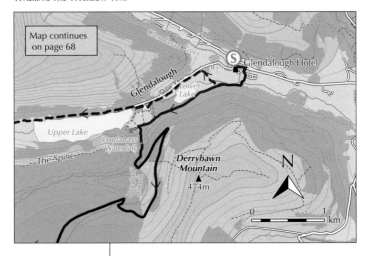

Map continues
on page 68

Note that it is possible to short-cut straight through the Monastic City.

Face the Glendalough Hotel and turn left as signposted along the road. ◀ Turn right into the grounds surrounding the **Glendalough Visitor Centre** and spot a walking trails map-board and a tarmac path. Walk as marked past a lawn to reach a Wicklow Way map-board and cross a bridge. The path rises to a junction, then turn right as marked and signed for the Green Road to the Upper Lake. A footbridge on the right offers one last chance to visit the Monastic City, otherwise keep straight ahead along the tarmac track. A point is quickly reached where walkers must decide whether to follow the Wicklow Way straight ahead, or fork right along a path to follow an alternative route.

Alternative via Miners' Way
Extra 2km (1¼ miles), 90m (295ft) ascent/descent, 30mins
The path to the right soon gives way to a boardwalk path crossing wooded and swampy ground, then it runs parallel to a road near the **Lower Lake**. The path reaches a car park where there are toilets and snack wagons. Cross the car park to pick up and follow a tarmac path through

The Upper Lake in Glendalough

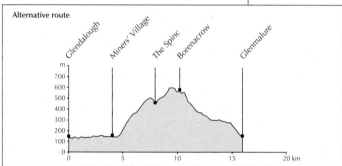

Alternative route

riverside woodland, turning right to cross a bridge. Turn left and pass a gate to follow a road through forest beside the **Upper Lake**.

The road serves an education centre, but walk straight ahead along a lakeside track, passing tall Scots pines. A sign draws attention to a view of St Kevin's Bed, which is a cave on the other side of the Upper Lake. The forest ends at the head of the lake and the track runs across a slope of bracken studded with granite boulders.

Lead was the main prize in these mines, though there was also zinc, copper and silver.

Reach an area of bright mining spoil and continue along a clear, but occasionally rugged path, passing the ruins of the **Miners' Village**. ◄

Pass between huge boulders at the foot of an impressive boulder scree, then hop across a little stream. Climb a stony zigzag path up a slope of bracken and boulders. There are waterfalls close to hand, with views back through the glen. The path can sometimes be stony, sometimes boulder-strewn and sometimes stone-paved, and there is a footbridge, as well as smaller plank bridges. Walk along a boardwalk path through a boulder-strewn area at a higher level. Turn left to cross a footbridge spanning the **Glenealo River**. Follow a path gently downhill, crossing a couple of small bridges to reach ruins and a noticeboard explaining about mining activities in an area known as **Van Diemen's Land**.

The path climbs stone steps, then after a gravel stretch, there are more stone steps and a stone-paved stretch. A footbridge leads onto a boardwalk path where

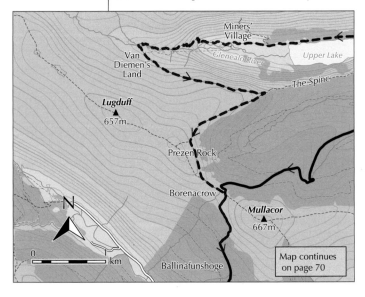

Map continues on page 70

the gradient is gentle, but almost 150 steps are climbed across a boggy slope. ▶ Descend 67 steps on the board-walk path to reach a junction and a marker post. Just to the left is a fine view of Glendalough and the Upper Lake from **The Spinc**.

Turn right at the junction and a short stretch of board-walk path beside a forest gives way to a path worn down to the schist bedrock. An obvious stony path rises fairly gently up a moorland slope, then it steepens. Turn left as marked at a junction and the path contours across a slope of grass, bilberry and heather, on the slopes of **Lugduff**, overlooking extensive forest, catching a glimpse of the Lower Lake. Pass quartz boulders above **Prezen Rock** and follow the path to a marker post. Turn left to pass between other wooden posts and walk straight downhill to pick up and follow a boardwalk path across a broad, boggy gap at **Borenacrow**.

The Miners' Way joins the Wicklow Way at a junction with another boardwalk path, around 560m, where a right turn is made.

Look back to see Turlough Hill, which bears a pumped storage hydro-electric reservoir. Closer to hand, look out for feral goats.

The Miners' Way and Wicklow Way boardwalks meet at Borenacrow

69

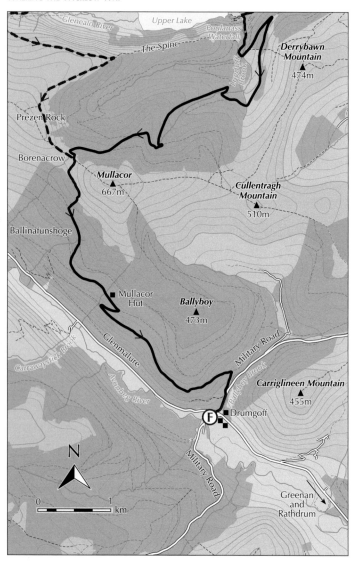

Upper Lake

Glenealo River

Poulanass Waterfall

The Spinc

Derrybawn Mountain
▲
474m

Prezen Rock

Lugduff Brook

Borenacrow

Mullacor
▲
667m

Cullentragh Mountain
▲
510m

Ballinafunshoge

Mullacor Hut
■

Ballyboy
▲
473m

Glenmalure

Carrawaystick Brook

Avonbeg River

Military Road

Ballyboy Brook

Carriglineen Mountain
▲
455m

Ⓕ ■ Drumgoff
■

N

0   1
                    km

Military Road

Greenan and Rathdrum

Looking towards Lugnaquilla on the forested descent to Glenmalure

Main route

Keep straight ahead and the tarmac track gives way to a broad, gritty path. The surroundings are mostly mixed woodland, with occasional views of the **Lower Lake**. The path leads to a junction with a tarmac path and the Wicklow Way runs straight ahead. Pass a national park information office, or pop inside if it is open. ▶ The route turns left afterwards, across a bridge, but it is worth making a short detour straight ahead first for a view of the Upper Lake.

National park office, 1000 to 1730, though often closed for lunch, tel 0761 002667.

Cross the bridge and walk up to a junction, turning left up 60 steps for a view of the **Poulanass Waterfall**. Keep climbing into the forest and turn left up a track to pass a barrier. Turn left again to cross two bridges. ▶ Follow the waymarked track gently uphill, and just as a junction is reached, catch a glimpse of Glendalough and the Upper Lake before turning sharp right. Continue uphill among Scots pines and observe marker posts at all junctions, as the route is remarkably convoluted near **Lugduff Brook**. Pass clear-felled and replanted areas of the forest and note places where native trees have been planted in favour of conifers. The track eventually reaches a turning area.

Note a display between the bridges, showing five rocks and minerals – granite, slate, schist, quartz and galena.

Lugnaquilla is the highest mountain in Co Wicklow, at 925m.

An 'Adirondack' shelter with three wooden walls, a roof and a floor, with one side left completely open. A picnic table and a fire ring are available outside.

Turn right as marked and follow a boardwalk path through a gate, onto a broad, boggy gap at **Borenacrow**. The Wicklow Way reaches a junction with another boardwalk path, joining the Miners' Way, around 560m. Both routes run in tandem straight ahead, with views across the deep, forested valley of Glenmalure, with the broad-shouldered mountain of Lugnaquilla rising beyond. ◄

The combined Wicklow Way and Miners' Way follows the boardwalk path down 45 steps. A well-trodden path continues alongside a fence, rising a little and passing through a gate. The descent is largely accomplished on a steep, clear-felled slope, using chunky slabs of lustrous schist as steps. Turn left at the bottom along a forest track, then later turn right down another track. The Miners' Way later turns right, while the Wicklow Way simply keeps straight ahead as marked. Watch out for the **Mullacor Hut** on the left. ◄

Soon after passing the hut, turn sharp right, then sharp left as marked at two junctions. There is a fine view across Glenmalure, taking in a waterfall and a zigzag path that offers access to Lugnaquilla. The track enters dense forest and loses the views, then later there is a marker for a path on the right, blocked by a boulder. Follow this path down to a barrier and a road, beside a bridge. Turn right down the road to reach a crossroads at Drumgoff.

There are three accommodation options at **Drumgoff**, and they can all fill to capacity on summer weekends, so it is wise to book in advance. The Glenmalure Lodge offers accommodation, food and drink. Notice the pikestaffs, a weapon particularly associated with the 1798 rebellion, used as flagpoles! The Coolalingo B&B lies roughly opposite the hotel. The Wilderness Lodge lies next-door and offers self-catering accommodation. When everything is full, Birchdale House B&B, 6.5km off-route at Greenan, offers pick-ups and drop-offs. If this place is also full, then the village of Rathdrum is 10km off-route. The Wicklow Way Bus, which must be pre-booked, links Glendalough, Glenmalure and Rathdrum: tel 0404 29000 or 087 817 6630.

DAY 5
Glenmalure to Moyne

Start	Glenmalure Lodge, Drumgoff, grid ref T 106 908
Finish	Sandyford Bridge, Moyne, grid ref T 036 791
Distance	23km (14¼ miles)
Total ascent	750m (2460ft)
Total descent	720m (2360ft)
Time	7hr 15min
Terrain	The main route mostly follows easy roads, forest tracks and paths, with several ascents and descents. The alternative route follows paths across open moorland and hillsides, with some parts being wet and boggy.
Maps	OSI Discovery 56 & 62, OS Adventure Wicklow Central and Wicklow South, EastWest Lugnaquilla & Glendalough and Wicklow South
Refreshments	Only at the start in Glenmalure
Accommodation	Glenmalure, the basic Mucklagh Hut, then sparse and off-route options around Aghavannagh and Moyne

Shortly after leaving Drumgoff there is a choice of routes. The Wicklow Way is largely confined to forest tracks and paths, while an unmarked alternative route is possible on the rugged and open slopes of Croaghanmoira. The alternative is worthwhile on clear, dry days when views can be enjoyed, but in poor weather it is better to stay in the forests. Bear in mind that there are no places offering food and drink throughout this stage, and apart from a shelter hut, accommodation is sparse and off-route around Aghavannagh and Moyne.

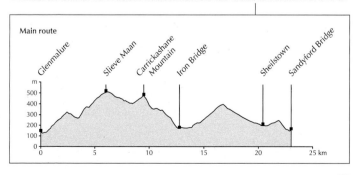

Leave the crossroads at Drumgoff by following the road signposted downhill for Aughrim. The road is known as the Military Road, and after crossing a bridge over the **Avonbeg River**, the derelict **Drumgoff Barracks** should be glimpsed to the left. However, the Wicklow Way is signposted on the right, along a track.

THE MILITARY ROAD

For many centuries the Wicklow Mountains were 'beyond the Pale'. While the city of Dublin was under English control, the glens were held chiefly by the O'Byrnes and they were well able to repel any forces sent into the mountains. In 1580, an English force was dispatched to Glenmalure and was roundly defeated, with Edmund Spencer and Walter Raleigh being among those fleeing for their lives!

It was in the immediate aftermath of the 1798 Rebellion that the Wicklow Mountains were finally brought under English control. Military forces were at a distinct disadvantage in such bleak and remote terrain, so steps were taken to tame the wilderness once and for all. Soldiers and navvies laboured over the mountains in the early 1800s, laying the Military Road over the bogs and around the mountainsides. They penetrated the remotest glens and built strategic barracks at Glencree, Laragh, Drumgoff and Aghavannagh. Each barracks building had a chequered history. The one at Glencree later served as a reformatory, then as a centre for Christian reconciliation. The one at Laragh was completely demolished. The Drumgoff barracks provided accommodation for miners and is currently derelict. The barracks at Aghavannagh became a shooting lodge, then a youth hostel, and now offers B&B accommodation. The Military Road is signposted as a scenic drive and offers access to several splendid walks throughout the Wicklow Mountains.

Follow the track across a concrete bridge and swing left to pass a granite post marked 'Halfway Point' on the Wicklow Way. Follow a forest track as it bends uphill as marked, avoiding grassy tracks in favour of the stony one. Turn left as marked at a junction in a clear-felled area, walking down a track to cross the stream called the **Cloghernagh Brook**. While walking downhill, catch a glimpse of Drumgoff through a gap in the forest. Watch for marker posts and two boulders where a path on the right, the Wicklow Way, climbs from the track. If the alternative route is going to be followed, then keep following the track ahead and downhill.

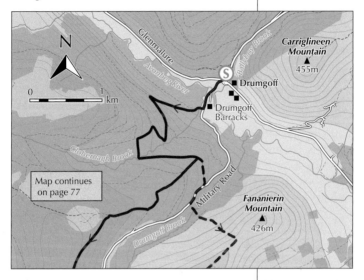

The granite 'Halfway Point' marker post in Glenmalure

Alternative via Croaghanmoira
Extra 3km (2 miles), 260m (855ft) ascent/descent, 1hr 15min

The forest track leads down to a barrier and the Military Road. Turn right to walk up the road, then turn left to walk down another forest track. This crosses **Drumgoff Brook** and quickly leaves the forest. Keep straight ahead to pass a gate marked 'private property', but note that immediately beyond it is a notice offering 'information for walkers'. Please read this notice, which basically explains that while the land beyond is part of the private Ballinacor Estate, considerate walkers are tolerated, and a route is outlined for them to follow. Also bear in mind that access might sometimes be curtailed in the interest of land management, or if shooting is taking place. Dogs and wild camping are not allowed. If access is unavailable please return to the Wicklow Way.

Pass to the left of the notice and spot a path running up a slope of bracken. It is vague in places, but basically climbs steeper and steeper towards a slight gap in view at the top of the slope. Three fences join at the top, on the crest of **Fananierin Mountain**, over 380m. Don't cross any of the fences, but turn right and follow a path parallel to the fence that runs along (or close to) the crest, heading roughly south-west. The crest gradually rises and is covered in heather, bilberry and grass, with some bare peat and rock exposed. A junction of fences is reached,

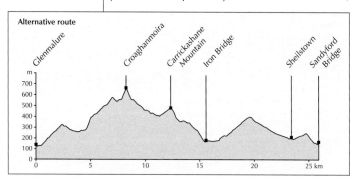

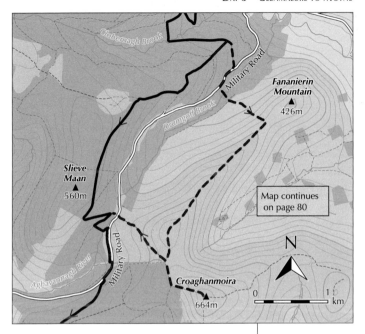

Map continues
on page 80

so step across and follow the path across open moorland on the crest, over a broad summit. Walk gently downhill to reach a path junction and pass through an old gateway near the corner of a forest. ▸

A path runs close to the edge of the forest, but this is really just a bulldozed firebreak, so use a parallel path on the moorland slope, passing the top corner of the forest and continuing all the way to the summit of **Croaghanmoira**, at 664m. A trig point stands on boulders of quartz and there is an extensive view around the Wicklow Mountains, along the coast, possibly extending as far as the Blackstairs Mountains and even the Mountains of Mourne on an exceptionally clear day.

Retrace steps down through the old gateway, then keep left to follow the path further down the moorland slope. Pass another 'information for walkers' notice and

If a decision is made not to climb Croaghanmoira, turn right and walk straight downhill. This saves over 1.5km (1 mile), an ascent/ descent of 115m (380ft) and 30min.

An alternative route could be taken to the summit of Croaghanmoira

The quartz outcrop can be seen even from the distant alternative route on Croaghanmoira.

another gate marked 'private property'. Cross over the **Military Road** on a crest above 450m and pass a barrier to enter a forest. The Wicklow Way is joined very quickly at a junction and is followed by turning left.

Main route

The Wicklow Way follows a boardwalk path straight up through the forest, reaching another track. Cross the track and follow the path up past a boulder that serves as a good seat. Later, bend left and follow the path gently down to a bend on another track. Turn right up the track and pass a prominent bright outcrop of quartz. ◄ Keep climbing up the track then turn left as marked at a junction and a map-board.

Climb more gently and look back to see Djouce Mountain and the Great Sugar Loaf, with Croaghanmoira closer to hand across a clear-felled slope. The highest point reached on the slopes of **Slieve Maan** is around 520m. The track descends and bends left, reaching a junction where the alternative route re-joins. Turn right as marked, although note that by keeping straight ahead, the nearby **Military Road** is quickly reached.

Walk down the forest track and turn left as marked down a boardwalk path. Leave the forest and climb a tussocky slope of grass, heather and bilberry. Turn right as marked and walk parallel to the Military Road, keeping just below it so that it is basically unnoticed except when a vehicle passes along it. When the path later joins the road, turn right to walk down it, then turn left as signposted up past a barrier, up another forest track. Keep straight ahead to reach a turning space, then continue up a path narrowly avoiding the forested summit of **Carrickashane Mountain** at 508m.

The path descends fairly steeply and passes the **Mucklagh Hut**. ▶ A view outside the forest reveals the scattered settlement of Aghavannagh, where the largest building was formerly a military barracks, became a youth hostel and now offers more luxurious accommodation.

Walk down a forest track, which bends left. Later, turn right when a waymarked junction is reached. Descend to a road and turn right down it, watching carefully to spot a signpost partly hidden on the right, which points left towards a barrier just below the road. Walk past the barrier and follow a grassy, stony track downhill.

An 'Adirondack' shelter with three wooden walls, a roof and a floor, with one side left completely open. A picnic table and a fire ring are available outside.

The Mucklagh Hut is located in forest high above Aghavannagh

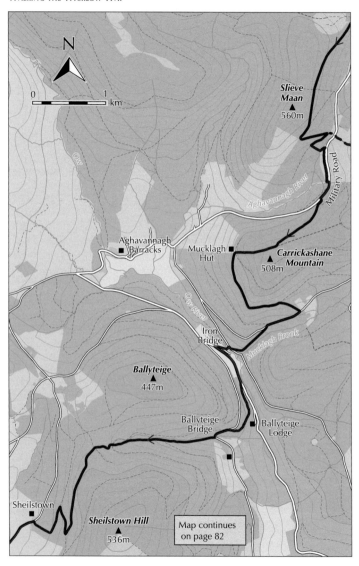

N

0   1 km

Slieve Maan
▲
560m

Military Road

Aghavannagh River

Aghavannagh
Barracks ■

Mucklagh ■
Hut

Carrickashane Mountain
▲
508m

Oxr River

Iron
Bridge

Mucklagh Brook

Ballyteige
▲
447m

Ballyteige
Bridge

■ *Ballyteige Lodge*

■

Sheilstown
■

Sheilstown Hill
▲
536m

Map continues
on page 82

A broad swathe has been kept free of forest in order to accommodate a power line. Turn right at the bottom, along a road, then quickly turn left at a junction to cross the **Iron Bridge** over the **Ow River**. ▶

Walk up to a road junction and turn sharp left as signposted. Follow the road until you reach a beech wood, also containing chestnut trees, and turn right as signposted up a forest track. (Keep straight ahead along the road to reach **Ballyteige Lodge**, which offers accommodation.) The track dwindles to a path while passing clear-felled and replanted slopes. Turn left along a road to cross **Ballyteige Bridge**, then turn right immediately and walk up another forest track.

Keep straight ahead as marked at junctions, and in the higher parts of the forest, the sprawling slopes of Lugnaquilla come into view. The track swings left, with views stretching from the western parts of the Wicklow Mountains towards the central plains of Ireland. Once the descent commences, turn right as marked down one track, then turn left down another track, which soon turns right and drops to a road at **Sheilstown**.

> **Avalanches** are very rare in Ireland, and deaths from avalanches rarer still. On the night of March 23rd 1867, after unusually heavy snowfall, there was an avalanche on the southern slopes of Sheilstown Hill, near Askanagap. The Mulhall family, six in number, were killed by it as they slept in a cottage around 320m. A memorial now stands where they died.

Turn left along the road and follow it past farms and houses, looking ahead to Ballycumber Hill and its wind turbines. Keep straight ahead as marked at a road junction. ▶ Keep straight ahead as signposted at another road junction, passing above the hamlet of Moyne. There are additional signposts for Kyle Farmhouse B&B, first along a road, then pointing right down a grassy track flanked by trees to land on a lower road. Turn left along this road, then turn sharp right at a junction and walk

The Wicklow Way Bus passes the Iron Bridge, linking Rathdrum and Tinahely, but it must be pre-booked, tel 0404 29000 or 087 817 6630.

Turning right along the road leads to the Airbnb cabin, Laurel Pod, 1km (½ mile), and the village of Knockananna, which offers a shop and pub, 3km off-route.

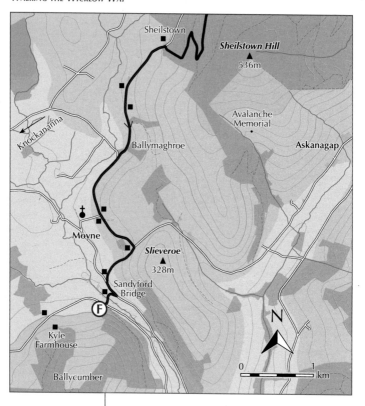

downhill to cross **Sandyford Bridge**. Climb to a complex junction and consider the next move.

Kyle Farmhouse B&B is reached by turning right up a road, for an additional 1km (½ mile), while the Wicklow Way turns left along the road, but offers no nearby accommodation. Anyone staying at Kyle Farmhouse might wish to continue the following day along an alternative way-marked route over Ballycumber Hill, rather than returning to this point to follow the Wicklow Way. Anyone struggling to find accommodation in the area could get a taxi to nearby Tinahely with Fiona, tel 086 815 7065.

DAY 6
Moyne to Boley Bridge

Start	Sandyford Bridge, Moyne, grid ref T 036 791
Finish	Boley Bridge, grid ref S 965 695
Distance	23km (14¼ miles)
Total ascent	490m (1610ft)
Total descent	540m (1770ft)
Time	7hr 15min
Terrain	Depending on route choices, a mixture of road-walking, farm and forest tracks, with some linking paths; some steep ascents and descents, but mostly gentle slopes
Maps	OSI Discovery 62, OS Adventure Wicklow South, EastWest Wicklow South
Refreshments	Plenty of choice off-route at Tinahely, The Dying Cow at Stranakelly Crossroads, off-route at Shillelagh
Accommodation	Off-route at Tinahely and Shillelagh

This stage begins with a choice of routes and there is also the possibility of venturing off-route to visit Tinahely, so be sure to be aware of all your options from the beginning. The Wicklow Way stays low on the slopes of Ballycumber Hill, while another route can be followed over the top of the hill. The Wicklow Way also stays well away from Tinahely, but some walkers might wish to visit and avail themselves of its many services. Those who visit the town may then climb Muskeagh Hill in order to return to the Wicklow Way. Facilities are sparse in this area, so some may wish to detour off-route at the end of the day to stay in Shillelagh.

Alternative via Tinahely
Extra 2km (1¼ miles), 230m (755ft) ascent/descent, 45min

This route would appeal most to anyone spending a night at Kyle Farmhouse B&B, just off-route from Sandyford Bridge near Moyne. The farmer has made a route available directly from the farm, marked with purple arrows often supplemented with 'Kyle Loop'. From the farmhouse, walk down the access road and turn left up a track, which passes above the farmhouse. It is obvious,

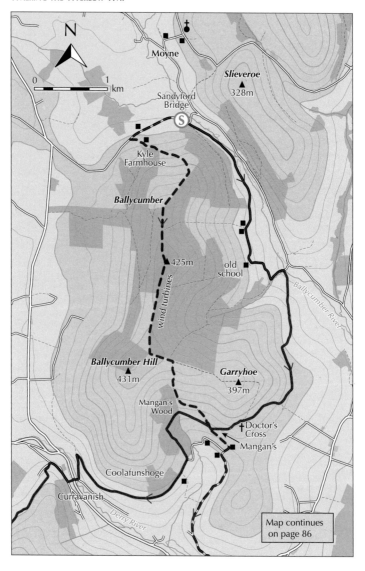

N

0   1
km

Moyne

Slieveroe
328m

Sandyford
Bridge

S

Kyle
Farmhouse

Ballycumber

▲425m

wind turbines

old
school

Ballycumber River

Ballycumber Hill
▲
431m

Garryhoe
▲
397m

Mangan's
Wood

✝Doctor's
Cross

Mangan's

Coolafunshoge

Curravanish

Derry River

Map continues
on page 86

grassy underfoot and offers fine views across the country-side to Lugnaquilla.

Forest rises to the right while fields drop to the left at **Ballycumber**, then on the higher parts there is forest on both sides, while a clear path is followed up a broad strip of moorland. Cross a ladder stile and follow an old forest track onwards, parallel to a broad, recent gravel road built to service wind turbines. A point is reached where two gravel roads run roughly parallel. Follow the one on the right, though it soon re-joins the other road. Follow the gravel road through the forest, passing **wind turbines** while crossing a summit at 425m.

Walk straight ahead towards a gate in a fence, giving access to fields. However, don't go through the gate, but keep to the left-hand side of the fence as marked for the Kyle Loop, and follow a grassy path between the fence and forest. Beware the electrified top strand of wire while passing the remaining wind turbines. ▸ Reach a corner on the forest fence on **Ballycumber Hill**, cross a ladder stile and turn left as marked.

There are views to Mount Leinster and the Blackstairs Mountains.

A stony path descends a heather slope parallel to the forest, with fine views. Turn right as marked at a junction and note that there are now coloured arrows marking three trails, which all follow the same path downhill. There is an abrupt change from heather to bracken and the stony path becomes a grassy path. Keep well to

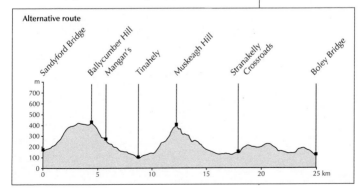

Alternative route

Sandyford Bridge — Ballycumber Hill — Mangan's — Tinahely — Muskeagh Hill — Stranakelly Crossroads — Boley Bridge

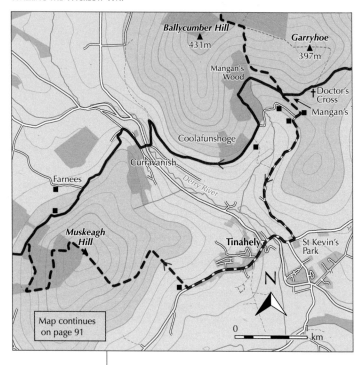

Map continues
on page 91

the left of a forest on the descent, passing other marker posts. Eventually, a track is joined in an area known as **Mangan's**. At this point, the Wicklow Way can be followed by turning right, continuing with the main route description. However, if the nearby town of Tinahely is to be visited, turn left to continue as follows.

The track leads to a gate with a ladder stile beside it, then it runs downhill to join a road known as Mangan's Lane. Simply follow this road as it descends past occasional farms and houses. It joins another road near the entrance to **St Kevin's Park** GAA ground. Turn right and follow the road across a bridge spanning the **Derry River** and follow Bridge Street up into Dwyer Square in the middle of **Tinahely**.

Looking towards Lugnaquilla while climbing above Kyle Farmhouse

TINAHELY

Tinahely was wrecked during the 1798 Rebellion, but is now a fine little town, boasting Georgian architecture, with three roads branching out from the central Dwyer Square. The square is dominated by the Tinahely Courthouse, which is now an arts centre. The town is the trailhead for a number of colour-coded waymarked walks, which are contained in a free leaflet – *Walking in Tinahely*, see www.tinahely.ie.

The town offers a full range of services, including pubs, restaurants, shops, post office, accommodation and an ATM. Bus services are quite limited, with a Thursday-only Bus Éireann service to and from Dublin. Wicklow Rural Transport buses operate on Fridays and Saturdays to Arklow, Gorey or Carlow. The Wicklow Way Bus operates daily, Linking Tinahely, Iron Bridge and Rathdrum, but it must be pre-booked, tel 0404 29000 or 087 817 6630.

Leave Tinahely by following Barton Street, to the left of Madeline's restaurant. Follow the road all the way out of town, off the end of the pavement, still passing houses, until a 'Welcome to Tinahely' sign is spotted. Turn right as marked by a red arrow for the Tinahely Loop. Go up through a kissing gate beside a gate and climb a little to reach two more gates. Go through the one on the left and an obvious broad, grassy path climbs steadily.

Watch for a step-stile on the left and cross it, then follow a grassy track across a forested slope. Reach a junction where a marker post indicates a stony track climbing steeply, eventually reaching a gate. Go through the gate and climb a little further to cross a step-stile. A grassy path flanked by fences and young forest climbs straight to the top of **Muskeagh Hill**, where there is a signal booster contraption on scaffolding, at 397m. Enjoy a fine all-round view of the surrounding countryside and hills.

Cross a step-stile and walk straight ahead, down a path beside a forest, on a slope of heather and bilberry. When a marker post is reached, turn left to cross a ladder stile and follow a broad path into the forest. The path turns right and descends steeply, then turns left to continue across the slope. Another right turn leads to another steep descent, and the path joins a track. Turn right and rise gently along the track, then simply follow it down to a barrier, where there is a Tinahely Loop Walk mapboard. There is a track junction just beyond, where a left turn continues along the main Wicklow Way route.

Main route

The Wicklow Way is signposted from the junction above Sandyford Bridge, near Moyne, along a level minor road. ◄ The road passes fields and woods, and the middle is sometimes grass-grown. When you reach a house and an **old school**, keep left of the latter and follow the road downhill, later noticing a memorial on the right for

A forest track could be followed instead, until a path leads back down to the road further along, marked by purple arrows.

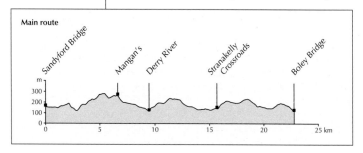

Main route

Sandyford Bridge · Mangan's · Derry River · Stranakelly Crossroads · Boley Bridge

Countryside near Stranakelly, seen while descending Muskeagh Hill

Luke O'Toole. ▶ The road leads down to a bridge spanning the **Ballycumber River**, but do not cross it.

Turn right as signposted along a track, which climbs past fields and is flanked by trees. Cross a ladder stile beside a gate to continue onto an open slope. There are hawthorns to the left and bracken rising on the right. The path is a grassy ribbon, occasionally a little rougher, but easy to follow and marked at intervals. There are a few gates with step-stiles alongside, as well as markers for the Wicklow Way, Kyle Loop and Ballycumber Loop. On a high part of the path, note the **Doctor's Cross** to the left and enjoy views of the countryside. ▶ Follow the path down to a track and turn right, noting markers for several trails in an area known as **Mangan's**. At this point, the alternative route could be followed left down Mangan's Lane to Tinahely, otherwise keep straight ahead along the track.

The track leads to a barrier and enters **Mangan's Wood**, descending through a beech-wood. Pass through forest and another beech-wood, then a gate and a

Luke O'Toole was a pioneer of the GAA (Gaelic Athletic Association).

The cross commemorates a doctor who was accidentally shot when his gun got caught while he was crossing a fence.

step-stile lead to a track junction. Turn right and go through a gate and follow the track as it passes through more gates. Emerge on an open slope of bracken at **Coolafunshoge** then the path later becomes narrower. Another slope of bracken is dotted with gorse bushes. An enclosed stretch of path leads to a track, where a left turn leads you down a road. Turn right to cross a bridge over the **Derry River**, reaching a signpost and a bench beside a busy road at **Curravanish**. (Turning left along this road leads to Tinahely in 2km, but beware of traffic. A pick-up can be pre-booked with the Wicklow Way Bus, tel 0404 29000 or 087 817 6630, or the local taxi, tel Fiona 086 815 7065.)

The Fairy Walk features a flight of 175 stout wooden steps

Cross the road and go through a gate to find the intriguing Fairy Walk. Climb 175 steps up a wooded slope to reach a signpost and a minor road. Turn right up the road, then turn left as marked and signposted, uphill from a junction. Turn left again up an enclosed path and go through a gate. Turn left up a track and go through another gate. Turn right along a grassy path, with fields down to the right and a gorse-clad hillside rising to the left. Go through gates as marked, later keeping left uphill at a junction at **Farnees**.

The path becomes rather rugged as it passes a small quarry on the slopes of **Muskeagh Hill**, rising to around 230m. The path leads down to a gate and joins a track. Turn left to follow the level track past a beech wood. Reach a junction and continue

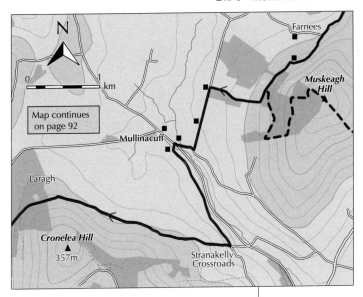

straight ahead. ▶ The track soon swings right to descend to a signposted junction with a road.

Turn left and follow the road through low-lying farmland to reach a signposted junction and turn right. Reach houses in the hamlet of **Mullinacuff**, where there are two signposted road junctions close together, so turn right at the first and left at the second. Simply follow the road through the countryside, but watch for little notices along the way that draw attention to features of interest. When the steep **Stranakelly Crossroads** is reached, Tallon's pub, also known as The Dying Cow, offers refreshment, but doesn't serve food.

Apparently, the police raided the **pub** one night, outside of licensing hours, and the landlady at the time defended herself by saying that she wasn't serving drink after hours, but was providing refreshment to neighbours who had helped her with a dying cow! The bar is tiny and there is seating outside.

This junction is where the alternative route, following the Tinahely Loop, rejoins the main Wicklow Way.

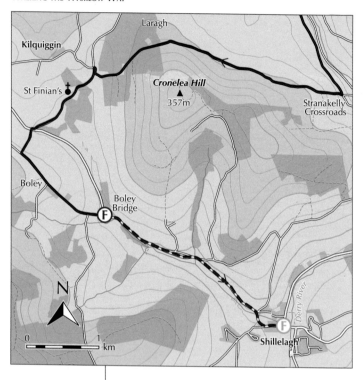

Shillelagh lies 3km away along a rather busy road, so it is worth calling for a taxi pick-up, tel 'Buggy' 087 946 9978.

Turn right and climb steeply from the crossroads, with a view back to the sprawling Lugnaquilla. The road rises, undulates, then later descends through forest. Reach a signposted crossroads where there is a house. Turn left and follow the road past **St Finian's Church** and a few houses near **Kilquiggin**. Reach a busy road at a staggered crossroads, turning right and left as signposted, to continue up a quiet road. Turn left at the top and follow the road past farms and houses at **Boley**, descending back towards the main road. Note that the Wicklow Way is signposted to the right at a junction before the main road, but if intending to visit Shillelagh, walk down to the busy road at **Boley Bridge**. ◄

SHILLELAGH

Shillelagh is well worth visiting for its services and interesting history. It is essentially an estate village founded by the FitzWilliam family, who at their height controlled one-fifth of Co Wicklow and had estates in Britain.

The term shillelagh is understood by most people to refer to a gnarled blackthorn stick that might well be used to inflict injury, and this is partly true. The history of the *Síol Éalaigh*, or descendants of Ealaigh, can be traced back to a 7th-century chieftain, but in turn he could claim descent from pre-Celtic tribes who always kept themselves apart from waves of invaders in this part of Ireland. They were essentially forest people, skilled metalworkers and stick-fighters. Their sticks could be used as tools, weapons, or even for transmitting information, if you knew how to 'read' the message. The most renowned

stick-maker in Ireland, Liam O'Caidhla, plies his trade in Shillelagh and exports worldwide. Visit his workshop, see www.oldeshillelagh.com, or have a look at the information posted in the local park, alongside an outsized shillelagh stick.

Shillelagh offers a small range of services, including accommodation, pubs, take-away, shop, ATM and post office, all contained between two notable buildings – the Church of Ireland, on an elevated slope, and the Courthouse near the Derry River. Local buses are operated by Matt Cousins, linking Shillelagh with Gorey, daily except Sundays, with Saturday services also linking with Tinahely and Carlow, tel 086 246 6264.

A monumental shillelagh stick can be seen in a park at Shillelagh

DAY 7
Boley Bridge to Clonegal

Start	Boley Bridge, grid ref S 965 695
Finish	Clonegal, grid ref S 914 613
Distance	19.5km (12¼ miles)
Total ascent	400m (1310ft)
Total descent	440m (1445ft)
Time	6hr
Terrain	A mixture of road-walking, farm and forest tracks; gently sloping hills
Maps	OSI Discovery 61 & 62, OS Adventure Wicklow South (part)
Refreshments	Pub off-route at Park Bridge; pubs at Clonegal
Accommodation	Off-route at Shillelagh and close to Clonegal

The final stage of the Wicklow Way is remarkably convoluted and it is quite likely that most walkers will start somewhere off-route, unless they organise a taxi drop-off. There isn't much scope for alternative routes, but if time is pressing, there is a short-cut worth bearing in mind, which could also be used to reach the only point of refreshment during the day – Egan's at Park Bridge. Once you arrive in Clonegal, a decision needs to be made about whether to spend the night there, or whether to attempt to leave the trail altogether, bearing in mind that time is likely to be limited late in the day. The latest bus leaves nearby Bunclody at 1350 (or Kildavin at 1355), except on Sundays, when there is a bus at 1750 (1755 from Kildavin).

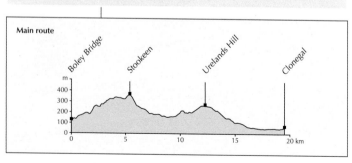

Main route

Starting from Boley Bridge, well outside Shillelagh, walk up a minor road signposted for Boley. Turn left at a junction, as signposted for the Wicklow Way. Follow the road downhill, uphill, downhill again, then uphill to cross a crest at **Raheenakit**, over 250m. Although there is access to a forest on the right, walk downhill a little before turning right as signposted along a forest track. All junctions inside the forest are clearly waymarked, and the way ahead is obvious, despite being convoluted. The route seems to run in every direction on its way across the hill of **Stookeen**, reaching around 350m. Clear-felling allows for good views from the highest stretches, including Lugnaquilla, Mount Leinster and the Blackstairs Mountains.

Watch for a marker post indicating a left turn down an old, grassy track flanked by gorse bushes. When a junction is reached at the bottom of the slope among fields, turn right to pass a farm and reach a road. At this point a short-cut is possible by turning left, otherwise turn right as signposted for the Wicklow Way.

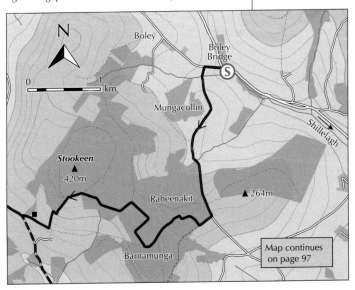

Map continues on page 97

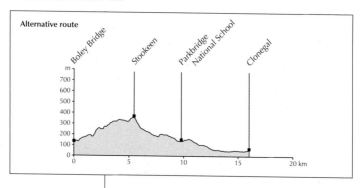

Alternative route

Short-cut
Saving 3.5km (2¼ miles), 70m (230ft) ascent/descent, 1hr

Turn left and walk down the road for 1km (½ mile) to spot an un-signposted track climbing on the right, before reaching **New Bridge**. ◄ The track climbs and turns left before becoming a tarmac road. Follow this onwards and it descends, reaching a road junction near the former **Parkbridge National School**. Turn right to walk up and then down a road, eventually reaching a signposted crossroads. The Wicklow Way is re-joined here; follow it by turning sharp left downhill.

The road could be followed for another 2km to Park Bridge and Egan's bar.

Turn right as signposted to follow the Wicklow Way along the road, then turn left as signposted down another road. This road undulates as it passes a few houses. Turn left as signposted at a road junction at **Money** and follow the road until **Forest Lodge** is reached, which is surrounded by a stout granite wall. Turn left as signposted, passing a gate to follow a forest track uphill. Turn right as marked at a junction on **Moylisha Hill** and note some fine beeches, rhododendron and honeysuckle beside the track. Reach another junction and turn right as marked downhill, bending left to climb gently. Pass more beeches and eventually reach yet another junction and a marker post.

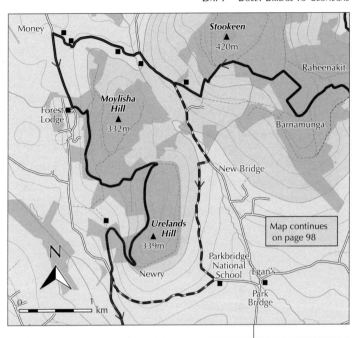

Money

Stookeen
▲
420m

Raheenakit

*Moylisha
Hill*
▲
332m

Forest
Lodge

Barnamunga

New Bridge

Map continues
on page 98

*Urelands
Hill*
▲
339m

Parkbridge
National
School

Egan's

N

Newry

Park
Bridge

0   1
          km

*The Wicklow Way passes through a
beech-wood before following roads*

97

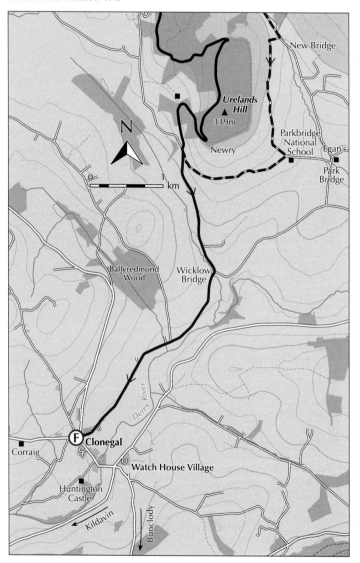

New Bridge

Urelands Hill
▲
339m

Newry

Parkbridge
National
School

Egan's

Park
Bridge

N

0   1
‾‾‾‾‾‾‾‾‾‾‾
        km

Ballyredmond
Wood

Wicklow
Bridge

Derry River

(F) **Clonegal**

Corraig

Watch House Village

Huntington
Castle

← *Kildavin*

Bunclody

Turn left and climb to a junction and a marker post, then turn sharp right along the highest track on the forested **Urelands Hill**, around 270m. The track gradually descends to another junction and a marker post, where there is a sharp right turn downhill at **Newry**. The track runs through a broad space in the forest where the margins feature a variety of trees. Pass a barrier and turn left along a track, walking through a beech-wood and continuing through an avenue of trees through fields. Reach a road and turn left as signposted, quickly reaching a crossroads where the short-cut re-joins the Wicklow Way.

Turn right as signposted down a road, eventually reaching a junction where there is a triangle of grass, with a signpost pointing right. Cross the **Wicklow Bridge** almost without noticing, passing from Co Wicklow into Co Carlow. Simply follow the road straight ahead past farms, fields and houses, eventually reaching a road junction in the village of **Clonegal**. To the left is a small garden that serves as the end of the Wicklow Way. Congratulations are in order, but before dashing away bear in mind that the village has plenty of interesting features and some thought needs to be given to leaving it.

Roads are followed through gentle countryside towards Clonegal

CLONEGAL

Clonegal was essentially an estate village attached to the rather secluded Huntington Castle. The public spaces are well-tended and the village is a frequent 'Tidy Towns' winner. St Fiaac's Church of Ireland and St Brigid's Roman Catholic churches are at the top end of the village, and the Carraig B&B can be found by following the road past St Brigid's, out of the village. Dunne's bar stands in the centre of the village, while the road running down to the Derry River passes the Wishing Well take-away, Foodstore, Sha Roe Bistro, Osborne's bar, with its coffin lid counter, and Siopa Uí Dhuinn (shop). A riverside garden features the Weigh House, where pigs were once weighed. An information board explains about points of interest, drawing particular attention to places associated with the 1798 Rebellion.

Huntington Castle is worth exploring before leaving Clonegal

Huntington Castle

Huntington Castle is signposted near the Sha Roe Bistro and an access road passes a gate-house, followed by a splendid avenue of mature lime trees. There are guided tours available, as well as a tearoom, gardens, woodland adventure park, and in the castle basement, the Temple of the Goddess. The Esmonde family arrived in Ireland in the 12th century and were involved in building a barracks here in 1625, on the site of an abbey. When the barracks were no longer required, they remodelled the building into their family home and successive generations have adapted and extended it. The current keeper of the castle is Alexander Durdin Robertson, a direct descendant of the Esmondes. For more information, tel 053 937 7160, www.huntingtoncastle.com.

Leaving Clonegal

Walkers need to decide whether they are going to spend a night at Clonegal, or press onwards to Bunclody, either to spend a night there, or to turn up in time to catch a bus from Bunclody (or nearby Kildavin) back to Dublin. It might be possible to negotiate a lift with your accommodation provider, otherwise, cross the bridge over the Derry River and follow roads signposted for Kildavin (4km) or Bunclody (5km, so long as you don't take the road signposted 'Bunclody 8km'). Cowman's taxi and minibus service is based in Bunclody, tel 053 937 7163.

The end of the Wicklow Way in the village of Clonegal.

Bear in mind that Bus Eireann 132, the direct service from Bunclody and Kildavin to Dublin, departs at rather inconvenient times. Departures from Bunclody are at 0600 and 0750 Monday to Friday, with an additional service at 0920 on Thursday, but only one service at 0750 on Saturday. Sunday services depart at 0850 and 1750. All buses depart from Kildavin five minutes after leaving Bunclody. The journey time to Dublin is 2½ hours.

Wexford Local Link buses depart Bunclody at 0840, 1040 and 1350 Monday to Friday, or 1350 on Saturday and Sunday. Again, these buses depart from Kildavin five minutes after leaving Bunclody. These services reach Tullow, where there is a 20-minute wait for onward Bus Eireann 132 services to Dublin.

Don't assume that these times will always be the same, but be sure to double-check the bus timetables in advance at www.buseireann.ie and locallinkwexford.ie.

APPENDIX A
Accommodation list

The following accommodation options are listed in route order. Places that insist on multi-night stays are not included. Note that inclusion on the list doesn't imply any particular recommendation by the author.

Many properties can be searched for and booked using www.booking.com; see also www.airbnb.com.

Day 1
Plenty of options in **Dublin** from expensive hotels to budget hostels. In order to stay within 10 minutes walking distance of Marlay Park, search Airbnb options.

Glencullen (1.5km off route, or on the alternative route)
Beechwood House
tel 085 727 8560

Knockree
Knockree Youth Hostel
(250m off route)
tel 01 276 7981

Ramblers Rest B&B
(2.5km off route)
tel 01 282 9539

Enniskerry (5.5km off route)
The Enniskerry Inn
tel 01 273 4992

Ferndale B&B
tel 01 286 3518

Day 2
Crone Woods
Coolakay House
(3km off route)
tel 01 286 2423

Pier Gates (options off route by road)
Lus Mór Hostel and B&B
(1.5km off route)
tel 083 311 7626

The Old School House
(2km off route)
tel 01 201 9929

Ashlawn B&B
(3km off route)
tel 087 902 5098

Roundwood (2.5km off route)
The Coach House
tel 01 281 8157

Riverbank B&B
tel 01 281 8117

Roundwood Caravan Park
tel 01 281 8163

Lough Dan alternative
Lough Dan House
tel 01 281 7027

Oldbridge
Wicklow Way Lodge
Oldbridge
tel 01 281 8489

Day 3
Brusher Gap Hut

Laragh (1km off route)
Bramble Rock B&B
tel 0404 45057

Lynam's of Laragh
tel 0404 45345

Wicklow Way Hostel
tel 087 092 0612

Tudor Lodge
tel 0404 45554

Riverside B&B
tel 0404 45840

Heather House
tel 0404 45157

Pinewood Lodge
tel 0404 45437

Glendalough
Glendalough Hotel
tel 0404 45135

Glendalough Youth Hostel
(400m off route)
tel 0404 45342

Day 4
Mullacor Hut

Drumgoff
The Glenmalure Lodge
tel 0404 46188

Coolalingo
tel 0404 46583

Wilderness Lodge
tel 0404 46839

Greenane (6.5km off route)
Birchdale House B&B
tel 0404 46061

Day 5
Mucklagh Hut

Aghavannagh (2km off route)
Aghavannagh Barracks
tel 0402 94477

Ballyteige
Ballyteige Lodge (300m off route)
tel 087 611 5016

Moyne
Kyle Farmhouse B&B
(1km off route, or on the alternative
route)
tel 059 647 1341

Day 6
**Tinahely (2km off route, or on the
alternative route)**
Derryview Farm
tel 087 903 4200

Murphy's Hotel
tel 0402 38109

Madeline's B&B
tel 0402 38590

Shillelagh
The Olde Shillelagh
tel 053 942 9113

Day 7
Clonegal
Carraig B&B (1km off route)
tel 053 937 7742

Huntington Castle
tel 053 937 7160

Bunclody (5km off route)
Meadowside B&B
tel 053 937 6226

Clody Lodge
tel 086 810 7136

APPENDIX B
Useful contacts

Getting to Ireland

Flights
Plenty of options, but check the following:

Dublin Airport
www.dublinairport.com

Aer Lingus
www.aerlingus.com

Ryanair
www.ryanair.com

Ferries
Irish Ferries
www.irishferries.com

Stena Line
www.stenaline.co.uk

Rail
National Rail (Britain)
www.nationalrail.co.uk

Irish Rail (Ireland)
www.irishrail.ie

Bus
National Express (Britain)
www.nationalexpress.com

Megabus (Britain)
www.uk.megabus.com

Bus Éireann (Ireland)
www.buseireann.ie

Getting around Dublin and Wicklow

Bus
Bus Éireann
www.buseireann.ie

Dublin Bus
www.dublinbus.ie

St Kevin's Bus
www.glendaloughbus.com

Wicklow Way Bus
www.wicklowwaybus.com

Wicklow Rural Transport
www.wicklowpartnership.ie

Matt Cousins Bus
www.cousinscoachhire.ie

Wexford Local Link
locallinkwexford.ie

Taxis
Dublin Airport and City
plenty of choice

Enniskerry
Kevin, tel 087 257 2973

Tinahely
Fiona, tel 086 815 7065

Shillelagh
'Buggy', tel 087 946 9978

Bunclody
Cowman's, tel 053 937 7163

Tourist information
Ireland
Discover Ireland
14 Upper O'Connell Street
Dublin 1
www.discoverireland.ie

Dublin
Visit Dublin
25 Suffolk Street
Dublin 2
www.visitdublin.com

Co Wicklow
Visit Wicklow
Town Hall
Market Square
Wicklow Town
www.visitwicklow.ie

The great outdoors
Wicklow Mountains National Park
www.wicklowmountainsnationalpark.ie

Coillte (Irish Forestry)
www.coillte.ie

Mapping
Ordnance Survey of Ireland
www.osi.ie

EastWest Mapping
www.eastwestmapping.ie

Emergencies
For the *gardaí* (police), ambulance, fire
service or mountain rescue, call 999 or
the European emergency number 112.

APPENDIX C
Irish place names

Irish place names are often highly descriptive of landscape features, so it is worth being aware of their meanings. However, bear in mind that many of the place names have been in use for hundreds, if not thousands of years, so they may refer to features that have long vanished from the landscape. Also bear in mind that many place names have been anglicised, so expect to find variations in spellings. The common Gaelic place name *doire*, anglicised as 'derry', refers to an oak wood, but don't be surprised to find it used to label a field where there are no oak trees in sight! Readers familiar with Scottish place names will notice many similarities between the languages.

Irish form	Anglicised form	Meaning
Abhainn	Avon/Owen	River
Achadh	Augha/Agha	Field
Aill	Ail/All	Cliff
Ard	Ard	Height
Áth	Ath	Ford
Baile	Bally	Town/Townland
Bán	Baun/Bawn	White
Barr	Bar	Top
Beag	Beg	Small
Bealach	Ballagh	Pass/Gap
Beann/Binn	Ben	Mountain
Bearna	Barna	Pass/Gap
Beith	Beigh	Birch
Bóthar	Boher	Road
Bóithrín	Bohreen	Lane
Breac	Brack	Speckled
Buaile	Booley	Milking place in summer pasturage
Buí	Boy	Yellow
Bun	Bun	Foot/End
Caiseal	Cashel	Stone fort
Carn	Carn	Cairn

Irish form	Anglicised form	Meaning
Carraig	Carrick	Rock
Cathair	Caher	Stone fort
Ceann	Ken	Head
Ceapach	Cappagh	Plot of land
Cill	Kill	Church
Cloch	Clogh	Stone
Cluain	Cloon/Clon	Meadow
Cnoc	Knock	Hill
Coill	Kil	Wood
Coire	Corry	Corrie
Corr	Cor	Round hill
Cruach	Croagh	Stack/Pile
Cúm	Coom	Corrie
Dearg	Derg	Red
Doire	Derry	Oak
Donn	Dun/Doon	Brown
Droichead	Droghed	Bridge
Droim/Druim	Drom/Drum	Rounded ridge
Dubh	Duff/Doo	Black
Dún	Dun/Doon	Earth fort
Eas	Ass/Ess	Waterfall
Éasc	Esk	Steep gully
Fionn	Fin/Finn	Fair/Clear
Fraoch	Freagh	Heath
Gaoth	Gwee/Gee	Wind
Garbh	Garriff	Rough
Glas	Glas	Green/Grey
Gleann	Glen	Valley
Gorm	Gorm	Blue
Gort	Gort	Field
Inbhear	Inver	River mouth
Inis	Inish	Island
Leac	Lack	Flagstone

Irish form	Anglicised form	Meaning
Leacht	Lack	Large cairn
Liath	Leagh	Grey
Loch	Lough	Lake
Log	Log/Lug	Hollow
Machaire	Maghery	Plain
Maol	Mweel/Meal	Bald
Mór	More	Big
Muc	Muck	Pig
Muileann	Mullin	Mill
Mullach	Mullagh	Summit
Poll	Poll/Poul	Hole/Cave
Ráth	Rath	Earth fort
Rí	Ree	King
Rinn	Rinn	Headland
Rua(dh)	Roe	Ruddy/Red
Scairbh	Scarriff	Shallow ford
Sceilg	Skellig	Rock
Sean	Shan	Old
Seascann	Sheskin	Marsh
Sí(dh)	Shee	Fairy mound
Sliabh	Slieve	Mountain
Slí	Slee/Slea	Way
Speanc	Spink	Point
Srón	Sron	Nose
Stuaic	Stook	Pinnacle
Suí	See	Seat
Taobh	Tave	Side
Tír	Teer/Tyr	Land
Tobar	Tubber	Well
Torc	Torc	Wild boar

Additionally, particles such as *an* or *na* can have the meaning of 'the' or 'of the'. Words ending in *-ín* or *-een* have the meaning of 'little', so that *bóthar*, meaning 'road', becomes *bóithrín*, or 'little road', in the sense of it being a narrow country lane.

LISTING OF CICERONE GUIDES

SCOTLAND

Backpacker's Britain: Northern Scotland
Ben Nevis and Glen Coe
Cycle Touring in Northern Scotland
Cycling in the Hebrides
Great Mountain Days in Scotland
Mountain Biking in Southern and Central Scotland
Mountain Biking in West and North West Scotland
Not the West Highland Way Scotland
Scotland's Best Small Mountains
Scotland's Mountain Ridges
Skye's Cuillin Ridge Traverse
The Ayrshire and Arran Coastal Paths
The Border Country
The Borders Abbeys Way
The Cape Wrath Trail
The Great Glen Way
The Great Glen Way Map Booklet
The Hebridean Way
The Hebrides
The Isle of Mull
The Isle of Skye
The Skye Trail
The Southern Upland Way
The Speyside Way
The Speyside Way Map Booklet
The West Highland Way
The West Highland Way Map Booklet
Walking Highland Perthshire
Walking in Scotland's Far North
Walking in the Angus Glens
Walking in the Cairngorms
Walking in the Ochils, Campsie Fells and Lomond Hills
Walking in the Pentland Hills
Walking in the Scottish Borders
Walking in the Southern Uplands
Walking in Torridon
Walking Loch Lomond and the Trossachs
Walking on Arran
Walking on Harris and Lewis
Walking on Jura, Islay and Colonsay
Walking on Rum and the Small Isles
Walking on the Orkney and Shetland Isles
Walking on Uist and Barra
Walking the Cape Wrath Trail
Walking the Corbetts Vol 1 South of the Great Glen
Walking the Corbetts Vol 2 North of the Great Glen
Walking the Galloway Hills
Walking the Munros Vol 1 – Southern, Central and Western Highlands
Walking the Munros Vol 2 – Northern Highlands and the Cairngorms

Winter Climbs Ben Nevis and Glen Coe
Winter Climbs in the Cairngorms

NORTHERN ENGLAND TRAILS

Hadrian's Wall Path
Hadrian's Wall Path Map Booklet
The Coast to Coast Walk
The Coast to Coast Map Booklet
The Dales Way
The Dales Way Map Booklet
The Pennine Way
The Pennine Way Map Booklet

LAKE DISTRICT

Cycling in the Lake District
Great Mountain Days in the Lake District
Lake District Winter Climbs
Lake District: High Level and Fell Walks
Lake District: Low Level and Lake Walks
Mountain Biking in the Lake District
Outdoor Adventures with Children – Lake District
Scrambles in the Lake District – North
Scrambles in the Lake District – South
Scrambles in the Lake District – South and East
Short Walks in Lakeland Book 2: North Lakeland
The Cumbria Way
Trail and Fell Running in the Lake District
Walking the Lake District Fells – Buttermere
Walking the Lake District Fells – Keswick
Walking the Lake District Fells – Langdale
Walking the Lake District Fells – Mardale and the Far East
Walking the Lake District Fells – Patterdale
Walking the Lake District Fells – Wasdale

NORTH WEST ENGLAND AND THE ISLE OF MAN

Cycling the Pennine Bridleway
Cycling the Way of the Roses
Hadrian's Cycleway
Isle of Man Coastal Path
The Lancashire Cycleway
The Lune Valley and Howgills
The Ribble Way
Walking in Cumbria's Eden Valley
Walking in Lancashire
Walking in the Forest of Bowland and Pendle
Walking on the Isle of Man

Walking on the West Pennine Moors
Walks in Silverdale and Arnside

NORTH EAST ENGLAND, YORKSHIRE DALES AND PENNINES

Cycling in the Yorkshire Dales
Great Mountain Days in the Pennines
Mountain Biking in the Yorkshire Dales
St Oswald's Way and St Cuthbert's Way
The Cleveland Way and the Yorkshire Wolds Way
The Cleveland Way Map Booklet
The North York Moors
The Reivers Way
The Teesdale Way
Trail and Fell Running in the Yorkshire Dales
Walking in County Durham
Walking in Northumberland
Walking in the North Pennines
Walking in the Yorkshire Dales: North and East
Walking in the Yorkshire Dales: South and West

WALES AND WELSH BORDERS

Cycle Touring in Wales
Cycling Lon Las Cymru
Glyndwr's Way
Great Mountain Days in Snowdonia
Hillwalking in Shropshire
Hillwalking in Wales – Vols 1&2
Mountain Walking in Snowdonia
Offa's Dyke Path
Offa's Dyke Map Booklet
Ridges of Snowdonia
Scrambles in Snowdonia
Snowdonia: 30 Low-level and easy walks – North
Snowdonia: 30 Low-level and easy walks – South
The Cambrian Way
The Ceredigion and Snowdonia Coast Paths
The Pembrokeshire Coast Path
The Pembrokeshire Coast Path Map Booklet
The Severn Way
The Snowdonia Way
The Wales Coast Path
The Wye Valley Walk
Walking in Carmarthenshire
Walking in Pembrokeshire
Walking in the Forest of Dean
Walking in the Wye Valley
Walking on the Brecon Beacons
Walking on the Gower
Walking the Shropshire Way

DERBYSHIRE, PEAK DISTRICT AND MIDLANDS

Cycling in the Peak District
Dark Peak Walks
Scrambles in the Dark Peak
Walking in Derbyshire
Walking in the Peak District – White Peak East
White Peak Walks:
   The Southern Dales

SOUTHERN ENGLAND

20 Classic Sportive Rides in South East England
20 Classic Sportive Rides in South West England
Cycling in the Cotswolds
Mountain Biking on the North Downs
Mountain Biking on the South Downs
Suffolk Coast and Heath Walks
The Cotswold Way
The Cotswold Way Map Booklet
The Great Stones Way
The Kennet and Avon Canal
The Lea Valley Walk
The North Downs Way
The North Downs Way Map Booklet
The Peddars Way and Norfolk Coast Path
The Pilgrims' Way
The Ridgeway National Trail
The Ridgeway Map Booklet
The South Downs Way
The South Downs Way Map Booklet
The South West Coast Path
The South West Coast Path Map Booklet – Vol 1: Minehead to St Ives
The South West Coast Path Map Booklet – Vol 2: St Ives to Plymouth
The South West Coast Path Map Booklet – Vol 3: Plymouth to Poole
The Thames Path
The Thames Path Map Booklet
The Two Moors Way
The Two Moors Way Map Booklet
Walking Hampshire's Test Way
Walking in Cornwall
Walking in Essex
Walking in Kent
Walking in London
Walking in Norfolk
Walking in the Chilterns
Walking in the Cotswolds
Walking in the Isles of Scilly
Walking in the New Forest
Walking in the North Wessex Downs
Walking in the Thames Valley
Walking on Dartmoor
Walking on Guernsey
Walking on Jersey
Walking on the Isle of Wight
Walking the Jurassic Coast
Walks in the South Downs National Park

BRITISH ISLES CHALLENGES, COLLECTIONS AND ACTIVITIES

The Big Rounds
The Book of the Bivvy
The Book of the Bothy
The C2C Cycle Route
The End to End Cycle Route
The Mountains of England and Wales: Vol 1 Wales
The Mountains of England and Wales: Vol 2 England
The National Trails
Three Peaks, Ten Tors
Walking The End to End Trail

ALPS CROSS-BORDER ROUTES

100 Hut Walks in the Alps
Alpine Ski Mountaineering Vol 1 – Western Alps
Alpine Ski Mountaineering Vol 2 – Central and Eastern Alps
Chamonix to Zermatt
The Karnischer Hohenweg
The Tour of the Bernina
Tour of Monte Rosa
Tour of the Matterhorn
Trail Running – Chamonix and the Mont Blanc region
Trekking in the Alps
Trekking in the Silvretta and Ratikon Alps
Trekking Munich to Venice
Trekking the Tour of Mont Blanc
Walking in the Alps

PYRENEES AND FRANCE/SPAIN CROSS-BORDER ROUTES

Shorter Treks in the Pyrenees
The GR10 Trail
The GR11 Trail
The Pyrenean Haute Route
The Pyrenees
Walks and Climbs in the Pyrenees

AUSTRIA

Innsbruck Mountain Adventures
The Adlerweg
Trekking in Austria's Hohe Tauern
Trekking in the Stubai Alps
Trekking in the Zillertal Alps
Walking in Austria

SWITZERLAND

Switzerland's Jura Crest Trail
The Swiss Alpine Pass Route – Via Alpina Route 1
The Swiss Alps
Tour of the Jungfrau Region
Walking in the Bernese Oberland
Walking in the Engadine – Switzerland
Walking in the Valais

FRANCE

Chamonix Mountain Adventures
Cycle Touring in France
Cycling London to Paris
Cycling the Canal de la Garonne
Cycling the Canal du Midi
Mont Blanc Walks
Mountain Adventures in the Maurienne
The GR20 Corsica
The GR5 Trail
The GR5 Trail – Vosges and Jura
The Grand Traverse of the Massif Central
The Loire Cycle Route
The Moselle Cycle Route
The River Rhone Cycle Route
The Robert Louis Stevenson Trail
The Way of St James – Le Puy to the Pyrenees
Tour of the Oisans: The GR54
Tour of the Queyras
Vanoise Ski Touring
Via Ferratas of the French Alps
Walking in Corsica
Walking in Provence – East
Walking in Provence – West
Walking in the Auvergne
Walking in the Briançonnais
Walking in the Dordogne
Walking in the Haute Savoie: North
Walking in the Haute Savoie: South

GERMANY

Hiking and Cycling in the Black Forest
The Danube Cycleway Vol 1
The Rhine Cycle Route
The Westweg
Walking in the Bavarian Alps

ICELAND AND GREENLAND

Trekking in Greenland – The Arctic Circle Trail
Walking and Trekking in Iceland

IRELAND

The Wild Atlantic Way and Western Ireland

ITALY

Italy's Sibillini National Park
Shorter Walks in the Dolomites
Ski Touring and Snowshoeing in the Dolomites
The Way of St Francis
Trekking in the Apennines
Trekking in the Dolomites
Via Ferratas of the Italian Dolomites Vols 1 & 2
Walking and Trekking in the Gran Paradiso
Walking in Abruzzo

For full information on all our guides,
books and eBooks,
visit our website:
www.cicerone.co.uk

CICERONE

Trust Cicerone to guide your next adventure,
wherever it may be around the world...

Discover guides for hiking, mountain walking, backpacking,
trekking, trail running, cycling and mountain biking, ski touring,
climbing and scrambling in Britain, Europe and worldwide.

Connect with Cicerone online and find inspiration.

- buy books and ebooks
- articles, advice and trip reports
- podcasts and live events
- GPX files and updates
- regular newsletter

cicerone.co.uk